Advance Praise for

The Rhythm of God's Grace

"Arthur Boers brings from the treasure of Christian tradition what is old and what is new, offering the ancient but ever-unfolding gift of regular morning and evening prayer to those who yearn to pray more frequently and deeply. As he invites contemporary people into this simple path of spiritual discipline and freedom, he serves as a wise, persuasive advocate and guide."

—*Dorothy C. Bass, author of* Receiving the Day:
Christian Practices for Opening the Gift of Time

"With the wisdom of a seasoned guide, Boers takes readers step by step through the logic, history, and theology of fixed-hour prayer. Story and practical counsel blend to create a rich resource both for those new to such prayer and those who long have practiced it. Boers shows how wise use of the daily office can bring beauty and reverence to prayer and can open the worshiper to a wide horizon of emotional and spiritual expression. Individuals and groups seeking deeper relationship with God will find inspiration in this book to practice patterns of devotion that originated in the early church and still unite a global faith community today."

—*J. Nelson Kraybill*
President, Associated Mennonite Biblical
Seminary, Elkhart, Indiana

"In this lovely, compelling guide to common prayer, Arthur Boers invites us all—from all denominations and levels of spiritual maturity—to be the Church at prayer *together* with the whole Church throughout time and space. This is a frank and very accessible introduction— with many practical tools to help us quarry and wear in practice the book's jewels."

—*Marva J. Dawn, author of* Keeping the Sabbath Wholly
and Teaching Fellow in Spiritual Theology
at Regent College, Vancouver, BC

the
rhythm
of **g**od's
grace

the
rhythm
of **g**od's
grace

**Uncovering
Morning and Evening
Hours of Prayer**

Arthur Paul Boers

PARACLETE PRESS
Brewster, Massachusetts

10 9 8 7 6 5 4 3 2 1

Library of Congress Cataloging-in-Publication Data
Boers, Arthur P. (Arthur Paul), 1957-
    The rhythm of God's grace: uncovering morning and evening hours of prayer / Arthur Paul Boers
        p. cm.
    Includes bibliographic references.
    ISBN 1-55725-325-0 (pbk.)
1. Morning prayer (Divine office) 2. Vespers. I. Title.
    BV199. D3 B64 2003
    264'.15-dc21

2002156456

Published by Paraclete Press
Brewster, Massachusetts
www.paracletepress.com

Printed in the United States of America.

Dedicated with joy, appreciation,
and deep gratitude to our children,
Erin Margaret
and
Paul Edward.

"Children are a heritage from the Lord,
and the fruit of the womb is a gift."
—Psalm 127:4, *Book of Common Prayer*

Contents

Foreword

ONE COULD PREDICT that it would only be a matter of time before someone would rediscover the ancient rhythm of daily prayer. That someone is Arthur Paul Boers.

His work *The Rhythm of God's Grace: Uncovering Morning and Evening Hours of Prayer* is not only a pioneer work among Protestants, but also a much needed primer for the whole church.

Speaking to our need, to the contemporary church's need to reapproach early church rhythms of prayer, Boers writes: "We can only know God's presence at all times if we set aside certain times for prayer." This is the sentence that jumped out at me, speaking clearly the key to the whole passion and burden of this book.

Fixed times of prayer, as the church has attested to throughout history, is in no way binding or legalistic. If anything, fixed times of prayer release our lives into the freedom of unceasing prayer!

But for many, and historically, this form of prayer has been lost. Though, and it has been interesting to watch, a warm change has come to worship and prayer for Protestants since the early seventies.

Why? It began with the liturgical church, simply, the · trickle-down effect of a document of Vatican II titled "The Impact of the Constitution on the Sacred Liturgy." This document encouraged the return to liturgical prayer, to fixed times of prayer. Word quickly spread within the liturgical churches. And by the late seventies and eighties, prayer books were developed within these liturgical churches to reflect a return to early church forms of prayer. A true sense of commonality and togetherness and ecumenism in prayer emerged and grew.

The impact among Protestants was slower moving. Yet a thirst for returning to the roots of the early church resulted. Growing toward the inevitable conclusion: There is more to the church than its Protestant history. Our common roots go deeper, and there is something we share with the liturgical churches. The quest for deepening roots has led some in the Protestant tradition to look toward the early and medieval church. The result? Many Protestants from the Free Church tradition have sought to recover the church's heritage in worship, prayer, and spirituality.

Attending to this desire for deep historical roots in prayer, Arthur Paul Boers has given us a book that introduces us to liturgical prayer, to its history, and to discovering ways to begin our own journeys of prayer.

I welcome this work and the sensitivity Dr. Boers shows to teaching daily prayer to those who know little about this great Christian devotion of the early church. The clarity, the profundity, and the challenge of *The Rhythm of God's Grace* will be of great help to all of us who seek to be more deeply aware of the intimacy with God established in prayer.

Robert Webber
Meyers Professor of Ministry
Northern Baptist Seminary

Acknowledgments

WITH THIS BOOK, more than any other, I am aware of a wide network that encouraged, sustained, challenged, and taught me over many years.

Michael David Lysack first introduced me to common prayer (Taizé's *Praise In All Our Days*), helping me to pray again when I was in grief. In my twenty-plus years of visits, St. Gregory's Abbey taught me more about prayer and worship than anyone else. I am grateful for the privilege of being an oblate there.

My last congregation, Bloomingdale Mennonite, gave me room and flexibility for studies, sabbatical times, pilgrimages, and above all, prayer. The Elders— Ray Boehm, Eleanor Snyder, and Myron Stevanus— supported my studies of fixed-hour prayer. Brave souls there joined my morning and evening prayer project, learning about and working hard at an unfamiliar prayer discipline: Pauline Bauman, Twila Lebold, Lorna McDougall, Sandra Mooibroek, AnneMarie Smit, Pauline and Richard Weiland, Linda Worth.

The Leadership Commission and Doris Gascho, the (former) Conference Minister of Mennonite Conference of Eastern Canada, granted sabbatical support.

Helen Kenik Mainelli (formerly at Northern Baptist Theological Seminary) was the single most important person in my Doctor of Ministry work on common prayer, consulting, encouraging, and supporting me from the beginning. Other key persons helping me there were Gerald Borchert and Robert Webber (who also gave invaluable publishing advice and encouragement). Peter Erb of Wilfrid Laurier University and Joyce Ann Zimmerman of the Institute for Liturgical Ministry led me in comprehending and unpacking key historical and theological ideas underlying the liturgy of the hours.

The Louisville Institute (funded by the Lilly Endowment) made possible my journey to Europe to visit innovative ecumenical and internationally influential communities, my visits to extraordinary monastic communities in North America, and my time spent writing this book. It is no exaggeration to say that its officers, Jim Lewis and David Wood, changed my life.

Various communities welcomed, inspired, and challenged me in Europe: David Adam and others at St. Mary Virgin Church; Ray Simpson and the Community of Aidan and Hilda on Holy Isle; members, staff, and guests at Iona; Brothers Jean-Marie and Émile and their community of Taizé; and *everyone* at Northumbria. I was grateful for weeklong visits at the Monastery of

Christ in the Desert (New Mexico) and St. John's Abbey (Minnesota).

My present employer, Associated Mennonite Biblical Seminary, also encourages me in my ministry of writing generally and specifically in encouraging the practice of the divine hours for the church today.

I appreciated the opportunity to test ideas in *Canadian Mennonite*, *Christian Century*, *Christianity Today*, the *Kitchener–Waterloo Record*, *CrossPoint*, *Reformed Worship*, and *The Mennonite*.

I am grateful to Biff Weidman and the Emmaus House community who welcomed me to morning prayers (when I awoke on time) during a hard transition. Other Anabaptists who particularly supported this project include: Hulitt Gloer, Nelson Kraybill, Alan and Eleanor Kreider, and Marlene Kropf.

Encouragement and good counsel came from Dorothy Bass, Eugene Peterson, and Phyllis Tickle. (And thanks too for their invaluable writing.)

Special thanks to Lil Copan and Lillian Miao of Paraclete Press, who blend professionalism and faithfulness into fruitful ministry. It is a great honor to be affiliated with a press that I have long admired.

Thanks to my daughter Erin for invaluable assistance in transcribing interviews and checking some references.

As always, the greatest thanks go to my wife, Lorna McDougall, and our children, Erin Margaret and Paul Edward, who are my three dearest friends and are graciously supportive of my work, studies, travels, research, and intense times of writing. Without them, not only would this work be impossible, it would not be worthwhile.

I am blessed beyond words.

Introduction

I DID NOT GROW UP LEARNING about daily morning and evening prayer. And yet it is an ancient tradition that goes back to the earliest days of the church and still continues to inform, inspire, and hearten many Christians.

Happily, we live in an era when walls that once divided the church are coming down. We are able to fellowship with, bless, enlighten, and benefit from one another. Many Christians look to the traditions and heritage of the wider church.

Years ago, I found that common morning and evening prayer help me overcome many difficulties and weaknesses of my own prayer discipline. These regular prayers keep reminding me that God is present, at work, and reliable. Thus such prayers call me to pay attention and to trust that God is active, even when I cannot discern God's activity for a long, long time.

Later, as a pastor and then a seminary professor, I wondered whether this way of praying could help others as well. I learned that many had no idea what it is, let alone what it might offer.

Yet at the same time I marveled when I saw people from various Christian traditions embracing traditional forms of morning and evening prayer, both in ecumenical communities and in church groups.

This book explores what this kind of praying offers.

In Chapter One, we consider basic understandings of prayer and look at why people are interested in the ancient pattern of fixed-hour prayer.

In Chapter Two, we look at internationally and ecumenically influential Christian communities, such as Iona and Taizé. Their morning and evening prayer is not only crucial to their identity and ministry, it also attracts others to them and empowers their powerful mission and outreach.

Chapter Three shows that such prayer is deeply rooted in the Original and New Testaments. Such prayer forms go back to the beginning of our faith and are a legacy that all Christians can claim, celebrate, and share.

What happened to this legacy bears much exploration, and so Chapter Four looks at the history of morning and evening prayer from the early centuries until now. Such prayer was distorted and lost by many Christians (especially Protestants), but still has much to offer all Christian traditions.

In Chapter Five we consider how to understand this way of praying, so that we can appreciate its importance.

An aspect of our culture that will gravitate *against* such regulated prayer is suspicion of and resistance to discipline, especially in the spiritual life. So in Chapter Six we reflect on the paradoxical freedom of disciplines.

Such prayer is not easy and thus in Chapter Seven we look at its hazards and obstacles.

Nevertheless, there are many blessings in this way of praying, as we see in Chapter Eight. It gives words to pray, sustains us in tough times, teaches us how to pray, immerses us in Scriptures, helps us deal with the challenges of time, connects us to other Christians ecumenically, and supports us in our prayer.

In the final chapter, we look at one small experiment with such prayer and how it enriched the faith and faithfulness of the members of a little church group, most of whom had never heard of it before.

To help you get started individually or as a group, appendices include practical resources. There you will find advice on praying morning and evening prayer, understanding its structure and content, and preparing and leading fixed-hour prayer for groups. Also included are recommended resources, both explanations and prayerbooks, to help you choose among the many possibilities.

It is hoped that this book will give you individually, or a small group of which you are a part, all that you need, practically and theologically, to begin praying some part of daily morning and evening prayer.

RECOVERING, DISCOVERING, OR *UNCOVERING?*

Sometimes I say that I want to encourage the *recovery* of common daily morning and evening prayer among those Christians (mostly Protestants, alas) that do not have it or do not know about it. The problem is that that phrasing assumes that Protestants had it and merely need to find it again. But by early on in the Reformation or soon after, most Protestants no longer did, although they may still have been influenced by it unknowingly. So "recovery" is not quite the right term.

At other times I say I encourage the *discovery* of common daily morning and evening prayer. But it is not possible to *discover* daily prayer. Such prayer was never entirely lost, even if some discontinued its use. We can no more discover it than Columbus "discovered America." Many Christians knew about the Office all along and still do. We do not *discover* their precious gift. At most we learn something that many other Christians knew all along.

The best way to describe and discuss this is to speak of *uncovering* common daily morning and evening prayer. Somehow many lost it, perhaps even buried it, but it is in the roots of Christianity, even in the roots of many Protestant traditions. What is required is not to find, invent, or discover something new. Rather we have the gift and opportunity to find what is already there and to claim it as Christians. It is part of our heritage, and it can be a great blessing.

I invite you not only to explore with me what happened to such prayer, but also to see what its potential can be for renewing our own spiritual lives and enriching the life of the wider church.

SHARING THE JOYS

I called a small group of people in my church to commit themselves to daily morning and evening prayer for the Easter season. Although this was new for them, most enjoyed themselves. Several experienced more gratitude, a deeper sense of God's presence, and an increased sense of purpose. Some commented on gladly learning the entirely new—but now obvious—idea of praying every morning and evening, addressing and greeting God at these key points in the day

As I grow more and more convinced of the gifts of such prayer, I long to share these joys with others. And in that spirit, I offer this book.

CHAPTER 1

Finding a Lost Treasure

Uncovering Morning and Evening Prayer

PRAYER HAS BEEN IMPORTANT TO ME since I was a child, when I began, with no direction or instruction from family or church, to read the Bible and pray daily.

For years I struggled to learn and practice such disciplines on my own. In high school I happily connected with other Christians who practiced what they called "devotions" or "daily quiet time." Many of my friends were committed to these disciplines, yet also struggled to maintain them.

In university, I am sad to confess, I had little tolerance for Christian traditions other than my own. Once, on a whim I bought a book by Jesuit Daniel Berrigan from the discard bin of a local bookstore. I saw that he took Scriptures seriously and his life, faith, vision, and activism were deeply shaped by prayer. I also realized that his disciplined daily prayer was a far cry from the "personal devotions" or "daily quiet time" that my friends and I tried to practice. We had trouble praying daily. When we did pray it was for just a few minutes a day.

Through Berrigan, I first saw a deeper Christian tradition of prayer and Scripture reading that many faith companions and I were missing. Such prayers are variously called the "daily office," the "divine office," "common prayer," the "liturgy of the hours" (referring to prayers at certain set times or hours), "morning and evening prayer," and "fixed-hour prayer."

Around the time that I read Berrigan, my sister and only sibling died of leukemia at age seventeen. This set off a huge faith crisis for me. Her death did not fit my cocky, self-righteous beliefs. I could not understand how God could allow such a terrible thing. And—this was particularly frightening—I found myself unable to pray and wondered whether I was losing my faith. At times I had nothing to say to God or did not know how to voice my prayers.

Then a friend showed me a Taizé prayer book, which gave me words to pray. It helped me voice laments and encouraged me to put my situation in a wider context. Slowly I learned to pray again. I relied on that book for many years.

Much has changed since I first skeptically read Berrigan. Now, as a Benedictine oblate, I have vowed to pray a version of the daily office and have resolved some inadequacies of how I once prayed. (Oblates affiliate with monasteries, promising to live their lives in a disciplined way according to monastic values.)

But I am not content. I suspect that the problems I encountered in my prayer life are troublesome for others too.

STANDING IN THE NEED OF PRAYER

When I was a pastor, parishioners often said they found it difficult to pray; they had no time or did not know how. It got to the point where I was actually *surprised* when an occasional parishioner said that he or she did pray every day.

I am concerned about the inadequacy of our prayer, especially in a culture that bombards us in many ways. Some may "pray" for at most an hour a week at Sunday worship and are *formed* by up to as many as twenty or more hours of television the same week.

I know the difficulty of being prayerful. Before learning fixed-hour prayer, my prayers were *ad hoc*: made up without paying attention to the Christian year or the priorities of the church and God's Reign or the needs of the wider world. They were *self-directed*: deciding on my own what I should pray rather than having help, support, or direction from others with maturity or experience, not to mention the wisdom of Christian tradition. They were *disconnected*: prayed in isolation from other believers, both nearby and around the world. They were *subjective*: praying what I "feel" like, freely abandoning important ways of prayer such as confession, praise, and intercession. Besides that, when prayer relied totally on my initiative and invention, it was easy to set aside when the mood did not suit me or if life circumstances were overwhelming.

Many problems of prayer could be addressed by a common discipline of daily morning and evening prayer. While this may be a new idea for many, it grows out of the history and traditions of Christianity.

THE SIGNIFICANCE OF FIXED-HOUR PRAYING

Prayer is about our relationship with God and involves all that we are and do in the context of that most important relationship. Because it is so important, prayer needs to affect our whole life, helping us dwell and live in God's presence constantly and encouraging us to be faithful while doing so.

But this is such a tall order, how do we do it?

Christian prayer needs discipline. Authenticity, informality, and spontaneity are often helpful, but they are not enough on which to base a life of prayer. Disciplined prayer has the possibility to inform all of life: thinking, acting, and doing. Various spiritual disciplines lend themselves to this priority.

Just as discipline is important to prayer, *daily* practice is also vital. Most spiritual guides insist on the importance of prayer happening every day. Yet many people are unaware of a classic Christian form of daily prayer. For millennia, Christians observed regular prayers during the day or even in the night. The primary services are morning (lauds) and evening (vespers). Their history goes back to the earliest centuries of the church. Various versions of such daily prayer—as many as seven or more services per day—can be found in Roman Catholic, Orthodox, and Anglican traditions, and there are some Protestant variations as well. It is no exaggeration to say that for most of Christian history, this form of prayer has been vitally important—and indeed still is for most Christians today.

Such fixed-hour prayer helps us pay attention to God and God's realities, "the deepest thing we know."[1] It embraces the whole of one's life. It offers consistent disciplines on a daily basis. Even its various names are revealing.

UNDERSTANDING THE TERMINOLOGY

One name, "Office," comes from the Latin word *officium*, which combines the two terms *opus* (meaning "work") and *facere* (meaning "to do"). "Office" then has to do with work, duty, task, and even responsibility.[2]

Fortunately, "Office" has other connotations as well. According to *The Compact Edition of the Oxford English Dictionary*, its meanings also include "something done toward any one; a service, kindness, attention." I think of such daily prayer then as a goodness done or given to God, an offering. Surely God merits our service, kindness, and attention.

Another term for this discipline, "common prayer," has several senses. It means prayers shared with other believers, as in the Anglican *Book of Common Prayer (BCP)*. The sharing and commonality can happen in the same place at the same time. But the same discipline prayed in different places is still "common." I use an Anglican prayerbook from a community in England. I have never visited there, but my prayers are in common with them.

Another sense of "common" is "ordinary." This prayer happens in the normal, routine, and mundane and thus helps place all of one's life in the context of God's purposes and Reign.

A third connotation is from the fact that the *BCP's* first author, Thomas Cranmer in the sixteenth century, hoped this kind of prayer would be again used by "common" people, not just the spiritual elite of priests, monks, and nuns.

Other terms—such as "divine hours," "liturgy of the hours," or "fixed-hour prayer"—remind us of a regular daily rotation of prayers (ranging from one to seven services) at certain set times. "Hour" is not just a time on a clock. An hour is more like a little church season. The hours, then, help us live and structure our time in a way that helps us pay attention to God and God's priority throughout the day.

This book focuses on morning and evening prayers. These classic prayers go back to the beginning of our faith. Not only strongly rooted in Jewish and Christian history, they are also the most accessible and practical for people today.

I use the terms "liturgy of the hours," "Office," "common prayer," "divine hours," and "fixed-hour prayer" interchangeably.

FORMAT OF MORNING AND EVENING PRAYERS

Morning and evening prayers take place in different Christian traditions. Sometimes the name tells you *which* tradition is being used. "Common prayer" is usually Episcopalian or Anglican. "Liturgy of the Hours" is Roman Catholic terminology. The "daily office" is often Benedictine. (Benedictine is not automatically Roman Catholic; there are Protestant Benedictines.) The "divine office" or "divine hours" tends to be Orthodox. Even though different terms are used, the services in all the traditions have much in common and are more similar than not.

No matter the name, all around the world, every morning and every evening, Christians in churches, private homes, monasteries, and other communities are praying similarly. All these prayers are more alike than different.

A simple way to look at morning and evening prayers is to see them as having a parallel threefold structure of offering praise to God, listening to God's word, and responding to God. (An outline of this structure can be found in Appendix B, Structure and Content of Morning and Evening Prayer.)

Morning prayer is often called "Lauds," which simply means "praise." Not surprisingly, praise is a high priority. In fact, the first words of this office are often derived from some variation on Psalm 51:15:

> O Lord, open our lips;
> And our mouth shall proclaim your praise.[3]

In many places, this is emphasized by making the sign of the cross on one's lips.

Then follows an invitation to praise and worship (perhaps as simple as "O come, let us worship"), a psalm of praise, possibly a hymn, and perhaps an opening prayer. Often, more psalms are read, sung, or recited. Psalms associated with morning prayer include 3, 5, 57, 63, 66, 92, 100, and 143. All are part of the first movement of morning prayer, bringing glory to God.

The second part of morning prayer is listening to Scripture. Here there may be a lot of variety. The lectionary sets different Scriptures for every day of the year. If one reads from the Original Testament, this is followed with a song of praise (canticle) from some place in the Original Testament other than the psalms (for example, 1 Samuel 2:1–8, 1 Chronicles 29:10–14, Song of Songs 8:7–8, Isaiah 2:3–5, Isaiah 9:2–7, Isaiah

12:2–6, Isaiah 40:9–11, Isaiah 43:15–21, Isaiah 55:6–11, Ezekiel 36:24–28, and Hosea 6:1–6). The Gospel of the day is then read.

The third part of morning prayer is responding to God's word. This is done in several ways. One may wait in silence after the Scripture reading, allowing its words and meanings to sink in more deeply. Usually one next sings, prays, chants, or reads Zechariah's canticle, called the Benedictus, from Luke 1:68–79. It cites a morning image in verse 78: "By the tender mercy of our God, the dawn from on high will break upon us."[4]

After that come prayers of petition that focus especially on dedicating the day and its work to God. The prayer is then concluded with the Lord's Prayer. Then the service closes with some kind of blessing.

Evening prayer, sometimes called "Vespers" or "Evensong," parallels morning prayer in its structure. (See Appendix B for a comparison.) While praising is still an important part of this service, Vespers also moves us to quiet down and be reflective—a fitting and appropriate agenda for the evening.

This office often begins with some version of the verse from Psalm 70:1:

O God, make speed to save us.
O Lord, make haste to help us.[5]

This opening response may be followed by a verse related to the time of day, for example, "Yours is the day, O God, yours also the night . . ." (Psalm 74:15) or "I will bless the Lord who gives me counsel; my heart teaches me, night after night" (Psalm 16:7).[6] Or see Psalm 139:10–11, Amos 5:8, or John 8:12.

In the first part of this service, it is appropriate to sing an evening hymn. A candle lighting or light blessing ceremony might be included. As in the morning, this is a place for psalms related to the time of day. A classic evening psalm is 141 ("Let my prayer be counted as incense before you, and the lifting up of my hands as an evening sacrifice"). Other evening psalms might be 4 or 16.

In the evening, New Testament canticles of praise are used (for example, 1 Corinthians 13:4–13, Ephesians 1:3–10, Philippians 2:5b–11, Colossians 1:13–20, 1 Peter 2:21–25, 1 John 1:5–9, 1 John 4:7–11, excerpts from Revelation 4 and 5, Revelation 15:3–4, or Revelation 21:1–5a).

The Scripture reading is followed in the evening by Mary's great hymn of praise from Luke 1:46–55, the Magnificat.

Evening prayers then focus on intercessions, lifting up the needs of others. This too is concluded by the Lord's Prayer, and then the people are dismissed with a blessing.

This overall pattern evolved over many centuries. When people refer to morning and evening prayer, they likely mean something very similar to this. But why consider such an old and possibly staid tradition?

TIMELY REFLECTIONS

It is now commonplace to note the current interest in spirituality. When I first attended seminary in the 1980s and did a thesis on spirituality, there were only two courses on prayer or spiritual formation. Since then, the seminary began encouraging students to be both trained as spiritual directors and mentored by spiritual directors, and it even offers a graduate degree in spirituality. (In fact, that is a program in which I now teach.) Times have changed and not just at that seminary.

Another place rising interest is evident is in the growing popularity of books on prayer. This interest is not just a desire for the new: People look to roots and traditions. Book companies notice that people are looking towards classical Christian practices. Phyllis Tickle, contributing editor for religion for *Publishers Weekly*, noted in an interview with me how one publisher described this as "rapidly hastening towards the third century." Books more and more are turning to early Christianity, not just before the Reformation but even before the church divided into East and West.

Uncovering fixed-hour prayer represents a return to ancient wisdom. It is a way of praying as did believers who preceded us, and even praying with them.

A RETURN TO ANCIENT MONASTIC WISDOM

As a part of this renewed interest in spirituality and return to ancient wisdom, traditional dividing lines are breaking down among Christians.

Protestants now look to spiritualities from before the Reformation sundered the Western church. There is great interest, for example, in Orthodox Christianity, Franciscan spirituality, Celtic Christianity, and pre-Reformation mystics such as Julian of Norwich, Meister Eckhart, and Hildegard of Bingen, to name a few. Even Counter-Reformation era mystics such as Teresa of Avila and John of the Cross get favorable attention from Protestants now.

Whether this return to earlier wisdom is the cause or the result of ecumenism is hard to say. But the reality of such respect and cooperation cannot be denied. During a Summer 2000 pilgrimage to England, Scotland, and France (which I describe later) I noted astonishing ecumenicity. Christians are crossing and uniting across former dividing lines.

Dividing walls are falling elsewhere too. One form of pre-Reformation spirituality getting increasing attention is monasticism. There is a Baptist Benedictine monastery, recently established in England. In

Minnesota we find history's first United Methodist monastery (also Benedictine). Consider the best-selling status of *The Cloister Walk* by Kathleen Norris or the surprising best-selling success in 1994 of the Gregorian Chant album by cloistered Benedictines. There is also an emerging interest in morning and evening prayer, a form developed within monasticism. In a conversation with me, Tickle told me the "surge of prayerbooks" in recent years is highly unusual; she knew of no other time when so many were published virtually at once. (See the bibliography for recent books.) The biggest publication surprise was a three-volume Office, *The Divine Hours*, edited by Tickle herself. The pricey first volume was quickly one of Amazon.com's best-selling books on prayer; within months the first 10,000 sold out.[7] Tickle was particularly surprised by the interest of certain Protestants who previously preferred extemporaneous—not written—prayers. Her memoir, *The Shaping of a Life*, reflects on her practice of fixed-hour prayer.

TAKE OUR MOMENTS AND OUR DAYS

Overlooking such prayer is at the least a tragic disservice. Given the long history of morning and evening prayer during most of church history and still predominating in much of the church, and realizing that it formed the background of many "spiritual classics," we ignore it at our spiritual peril.

It should not be an obligation for all Christians. (Office practices have sometimes been harmed by such unhealthy demands.) Even eloquent advocates of this kind of prayer admit that it is not for everyone. Nevertheless the "lost treasure" of a daily office has much to offer. This way of prayer can help some—perhaps many—to pray. To paraphrase a great old hymn, "Take my life and let it be," this is a way for God to "take our moments and our days; let them flow in ceaseless praise. . . ."[8]

CHAPTER 2

Uncommon Prayer

Morning and Evening Prayer in Diverse Communities

FROM REFLECTING ON MY OWN PRACTICE of common prayer and then reading what others say about it, my ideas grew slowly. Unfortunately, much of my experience was in isolation, as many in my church tradition are unfamiliar with this practice.

I wanted to know how various Christian communities pray this prayer. So in the summer of 2000, I traveled to Europe to visit communities that I had long admired. I knew them to be significant places of prayer and retreat. I appreciated their ecumenical influence and was astounded by their fame around the world. I went to experience their daily morning and evening prayer.

BASEMENT PRAISE

My first evening on Lindisfarne (also known as Holy Isle) in northern England, I noticed a sign on a nearby building, welcoming visitors to "night prayer" with the Community of Aidan and Hilda. I decided to

15

attend and see what there was to be discovered. After all, the purpose of my trip was to explore people's common prayer. I ended up liking it so much that I attended each night of the week.

Worship was an unexpected blend of influences. We sang hymns and choruses, with the basses booming deeply and reverberating pleasingly. Everyone shared Bible readings. There was space for personalized intercessions. Once a week there was the laying on of hands for healing. Some spoke in tongues and others raised their hands in praise. I was delighted by the eclectic mix of Anglican, charismatic, evangelical, Celtic, Catholic, and Orthodox worship elements, a combination I had never encountered in North America.

Who are these people? I wondered. Later I learned they were nationally known charismatic Christians who had come to appreciate their Celtic heritage. My mystification is a good reminder of one gift of fixed-hour prayer: Geographically, theologically, denominationally, and temperamentally diverse Christians can be united by it.

After each service, there was interaction among participants: sometimes simple conversations over tea, once a deep discussion about suffering and God's existence, sometimes ministering to a particular need. All of this confirmed that these services touched people's hearts and deepened aspects of their faith.

A PLACE OF PILGRIMAGE AND PRAYER

Lindisfarne has been an important place of pilgrimage for hundreds of years. Apparently, Alcuin, the medieval archbishop and scholar, told Charlemagne it was "the holiest place in all of England." Numerous Celtic Christian saints are associated with it, and the gloriously illustrated Celtic manuscript, the eighth-century Lindisfarne Gospels, also came from here.

The island's oldest building, St. Mary Virgin Church (Anglican), sees 148,000 visitors each year. Its architecture reflects both Saxon and Norman influences, some of it from before the twelfth century. Each day, St. Mary's celebrates morning and evening prayers and communion. Knowing that people had prayed in this place for over a millennium gave me a strong sense of tradition and the communion of saints.

I had not anticipated how cold this location in the North Sea would be. Every day I wished I had gloves and long johns, even though it was July. In each service, the half dozen or so people stayed bundled up in warm clothes and winter coats. Yet I loved praying between these ancient walls while hearing the winds howl outside. Jesus said the Spirit is like the wind in that it "blows where it chooses," and those winds reminded me of Pentecost. (One of the earliest names for this place literally meant "island of the strong winds.")

Services were "by the book," and the book was the Anglican *Alternative Services*. Everything was according to Anglican common prayer. Participants sat in the choir chancel, and each side of the choir took turns praying aloud a verse from the psalms, slowly and meditatively.

St. Mary's pastor, David Adam, has authored over a dozen books of Celtic Christian prayers, including *The Rhythm of Life: Celtic Daily Prayer*, an Office. He wrote this for the many people, including Anglicans, who are unfamiliar with traditional daily prayer. Its short prayers and Scriptures can be memorized quickly, so those who use it can be nourished at all times and places.

Adam told me that since beginning his Holy Isle ministry, he's seen a "great searching in people." Many want guidance on prayer. He meets as many visitors as possible and offers counsel, support, and advice. He encourages people to pray at the same time as the services at St. Mary's, "so that they feel they've got a link." He also invites people to keep in touch by mail so he can continue to give spiritual support.

In Adam's ministry I saw something that was confirmed in each community I visited. Even though not all came away committed to a full-blown version of the morning and evening Office, they were drawn to a deeper life of prayer. And it was each community's rootedness in common fixed-hour prayer that helped give it important resources in its ministry.

HUMMING HYMNS AND CLEANING TOILETS

Next I went to Iona, a small island off Scotland's west coast. Columba, an Irish monk, landed there in the sixth century and set up a monastic base that eventually evangelized much of Scotland, England, and Europe. The monastery is known for a beautifully illustrated Celtic manuscript, *The Book of Kells*. The island's sense of history is further reinforced by ancient gravestones and standing crosses (one over 1,000 years old). Samuel Johnson once wrote that a person "is little to be envied whose piety would not grow warmer among the ruins of Iona." It is a stunning place with stark hills, huge boulders, snow-white beaches, and many-hued waters.

In the 1930s, the Church of Scotland (Presbyterian) clergyman George MacLeod gathered seminary students and tradesmen to rebuild the ruined medieval abbey. In this project ministers learned to understand working-class folk, while those working-class tradespeople learned how to do theology. It was the beginning of the Iona Community. Now with more than 200 members from many denominations, and growing steadily, the community has a strong commitment to peace and justice and is known for its worship resources. Its conferences are so popular that reservations must be made months in advance.

I stayed a week at the abbey. The hinges of each day were daily morning and evening prayer. These prayer times were of utmost importance, so that—as we were told at orientation—the "day is held in prayer."

Worship and work were integrated. Morning worship never ends with a closing blessing—as the work that follows is part of the worship—and the evening service never begins with a call to worship (the traditional opening prayer of a worship service), since it is an extension of worshipful work. There is a strong emphasis on community and chore-sharing. Each day I proceeded from attending morning prayers to cleaning toilets while still humming hymns.

Services ranged from liturgical and contemplative—evoking Iona's monastic heritage—to lively and inspiring, sometimes reminding me of revival meetings when we clapped enthusiastically to old gospel tunes. We said the Lord's Prayer (each in our most familiar language) rhythmically, phrase by phrase, every line echoing against the stone walls like the waves beating on rocks a few hundred feet away. The singing included praise choruses, hymns, African-American spirituals, monastic chants, and international Christian music— all in the magnificent acoustics of the rebuilt medieval church. Prayers are continually being written and modified by community members, with simple, vivid language that communicates richly today but also taps into long-standing Christian traditions.

ANTICIPATING HEAVEN

During the hot July week that followed, I visited the Taizé community in Southern France. There were more than 4,500 other pilgrims there too, mostly young adults from many denominations and 60 nations (including a thousand from Eastern Europe). Summer weeks typically see between 2,500 and 6,000 visitors, with a total of 100,000 per year.

Taizé was founded by Brother Roger during World War Two. Of Reformed background, he intended this to be a prayerful ecumenical community to reconcile Christians from different traditions, especially after the horrors of World War Two. Taizé has a worldwide ecumenical reputation, and its worship is influenced by many traditions, especially Roman Catholicism and Orthodoxy.

Taizé's only impressive building is the church, appropriately enough, the Taizé brothers would say. Every day is organized around three worship services—morning, noon, and evening, each lasting an hour. People sit or kneel in a darkened room, facing ceiling-to-floor banners, hundreds of flickering candles, and several large icons. Music is led by an unseen song leader and a volunteer choir. Each service is a series of Taizé chants, short Bible readings (especially from the Psalms and the Gospels), prayers (translated into four to six languages), and a deep silence of five to ten minutes (no mean feat with thousands of young people). The emphasis in the daily services is on simplicity (which is especially necessary given the different language groups and church traditions) and on evoking mystery and reverence.

And it works. The singing was so beautiful that for the first time in my life I was attracted to the idea of singing in heaven for all eternity, in spite of my weak voice. When the evening service ended at 9:20, many opted to sing and pray for hours more, often past midnight. Some deep need was being touched.

INTERCESSION AND A LEAKY ROOF

I visited next a much less known place, the Northumbria Community. Its symbolic center is Hetton Hall, an old, rambling house in remote, rural northern England, built around a thirteenth-century tower. The community is friendly and informal. (The pay phone could not be used as it was jammed full of change, and no one knew where the key was to open it.)

Years ago, the publishing giant Harper got hold of Northumbria's prayerbook and sought permission to publish it. *Celtic Daily Prayer* sold well, and as a result of seeing the prayerbook people have come from the United States, Canada, France, Australia, and Russia to visit. The community is surprised at the response.

I detected more of an evangelical flavor here than in other communities, especially in their willingness to share personally and to pray for one another's specific needs. In spite of the evangelicalism, there were icons everywhere, and rooms were named after Celtic and Anglo-Saxon saints. The community is enriched by many Christian traditions.

They pray together four times a day. Their chapel is a rough wooden structure. Its roof often leaks rainwater onto the hymnals. Their Office is liturgical, with elements of Celtic imagery. They sing hymns and choruses. And there is ample time for sharing, especially of prayer concerns.

This is a place of ministry, healing, and growth. As in the other communities I visited, members feel a particular call to reach out to those who are skeptical of the established church.

Visitors spoke of how Northumbria helped them in their faith. A Baptist member first found liturgical worship foreign, but saw that it affirmed "other truths, I need to hear." She particularly appreciated the Office's connection with other Christian traditions.

Community member Rob Brown told me that even nonliturgical people find "anchors" in fixed-hour prayer: "For people in deep struggles, to have something that happens every day at the same time is like a skeleton that keeps them from falling to pieces."

ALL PRAYERS JOINED INTO ONE

More recently, on this side of the ocean, I stayed at the Monastery of Christ in the Desert in New Mexico for a week. It is in the wilderness, thirteen miles from the nearest paved road, in a strikingly beautiful location. As one expects in the desert, the sun was blazing hot. But thick adobe church walls provided some relief. On feast days, citrus-smelling incense wafted about, stirred by the hot desert wind blowing in through open doors. Often there were a dozen monks, Asian, Latino, and white. Sometimes as they chanted they were off tune, poorly coordinated, and not in unison. But in spite of occasional fumbling, they conveyed a sense of deep reverence and awe.

As I sat praying with them, even though I had never been there before and it was a unique location, suddenly the entire service seemed familiar. This was so in spite of the fact that they often sang and prayed in Latin.

While sitting there, I felt connected to all the places in which I had prayed previously, certainly Aidan and Hilda, St. Mary the Virgin Church, Iona, Taizé, and Northumbria. I also recalled monasteries I've visited here in North America, whether the Anglican St. Gregory's Abbey in Three Rivers, Michigan (where I am an oblate), the Trappist Abbeys of Gethsemane in Kentucky (made famous by Thomas Merton) and Genesee in New York (written about by my spiritual father, Henri Nouwen), St. Meinrad Archabbey in Indiana (where I heard the best monastic singing ever), or the Cistercian Monastery of Notre Dame in Ontario (sadly, now closed). I even vividly relived praying Vespers with Greek Orthodox monks in a remote region of Syria, and praying in English, Coptic, Arabic, and Greek with friends at St. Mary's Coptic Orthodox Church, near my former home in Kitchener.

All that praying and worshiping was joined together no matter where I happened to be, no matter the language or church tradition, no matter even the different liturgical and worship style. Reformed, evangelical, charismatic, Anglican, Trappist, Benedictine, Coptic Orthodox, Greek Orthodox, and nondenominational were all deeply united in these services.

It was not just that these people were all Christians. Or that they were worshiping. Their commonality went deeper: Their services were similar. They all prayed in the morning and in the evening. They used common psalms, canticles, and hymns. They regularly used particular themes of praise, confession, and intercession. No matter their race, country, location, denomination, or liturgical preference, they had far more in common than not.

All these communities practiced a form of fixed-hour prayer, a tradition that goes back to the beginning of Christian history. And I long for a deeper appreciation by more fellow Christians for this rich way of praying.

SEEKERS AND THE OFFICE

All these places of prayer say their common discipline of daily morning and evening prayer is central to their worship and service. The atmosphere of prayer that is formed by such a practice is an essential reason for which they are influential, are able to minister, and draw so much attendance and attention.

Strikingly, Lindisfarne, Iona, Taizé, and Northumbria are off the beaten path and are difficult to reach. Accommodations are rough. There are no shopping malls, video outlets, movie theaters, waterslides, or coffee shops. Yet the numbers are astounding. People of all church stripes and even no church connections come from around the world. Here is good news in a time of spiritual searching.

Ray Simpson, leader of the Community of Aidan and Hilda, spoke with me about common prayer today. Like David Adam, he meets many people who come to Holy Isle seeking. They are "fed up with churches that are task driven" and long for "something more organic, rhythmic," especially a rhythm of prayer. Yet, he observes, while many "churches are locked," no longer available for prayer, "houses of prayer are growing and becoming alive." There are more prayer and retreat centers than ever.

In a time of pilgrimage, when people look to ancient Christian resources (or elsewhere when we do not provide them) and struggle with deep questions, the church must respond. Common prayer helped form the many refuges of prayer described here and offers great promise in creating other sanctuaries too where people can be supported in their prayer, even in their yearning for prayer.

While the level of interest may be new, these prayer forms are not, but are rooted already in ancient biblical traditions. Since such ancient prayer forms are dramatically relevant, we turn now from my twenty-first century pilgrimage to the very foundations of this kind of prayer.

CHAPTER 3

Ancient Rhythms
of Prayer

*Biblical Roots of Morning
and Evening Prayer*

IT IS AMAZING HOW ONE can miss something that is right in front of one's eyes. Growing up in Southern Ontario, I assumed that interesting birds were found elsewhere in the world. I thought all local birds were small to medium and mostly black, brown, or gray. Colorful birds such as parrots, large ones such as eagles, or particularly striking birds such as storks must live in warmer, more exotic climates.

Perhaps I was misled by reliance on nature shows and their easy revelation of intriguing vistas in faraway places. *Wild Kingdom* was a popular television show then. Maybe it was my lack of interest in science. On the other hand, I have never been particularly observant.

Years later, when I lived in Indiana for the first time, I went for daily walks through a nearby park along a river. One day, for some reason, a friend loaned me a camera zoom lens and I took it with me. I used it to look more closely at trees, bushes, and the riverbank.

My walk was a lot slower that day, and thereafter too, because I discovered a bird cornucopia that I had no idea existed. I saw iridescent Indigo Buntings, magisterial Blue Herons, improbably amusing Northern Flickers, colorful Rufous-sided Towhees, and stunning Rose-breasted Grosbeaks, to name just a few common *and* beautiful birds. Some time later, I was in Southern Ontario near where I was raised, and went birding. To my shock and embarrassment, all those wonderful birds and more were there, too. Yet I had somehow missed them while growing up.

Something similar happened once I started studying the discipline of common morning and evening prayer. It became clear that this practice was rooted in familiar Bible passages, and yet I had never seen it before.

PRAISING GOD IN AND THROUGH THE PSALMS

Christians have often called the psalms "the prayer book of the church." Many different Christians throughout the centuries have relied on psalms for prayer, more than on any other source. In the church where I was raised, we sang from something called a *Psalter* because in it all the psalms were put to music. Most hymns were based directly on psalms. When this church added other hymns early in the last century, many believers—including my grandfather—were deeply offended. Hymns were seen as too superficial and not particularly biblical. Worship wars in one guise or another have gone on for a long time. The stakes have been high because the psalms are central and foundational to our worship and prayer.

The psalms, of course, were originally the prayer and worship book of the Jews, who still treasure it. The first Christians (even before they were called or called themselves "Christian") prayed as Jews. So they too relied on psalms for their prayer and worship. To this day, common morning and evening prayer relies heavily on psalms. Each service begins by praying two or three psalms.

These important texts do not just give us prayer content but also teach us much about a biblical view of prayer.

First, psalms indicate that God is always and everywhere mysteriously present. Psalm 139 says that God is present in the womb, in heaven, and "at the farthest limits of the sea."

Paradoxically, according to Psalm 139, God is even present where it feels as if God is absent: in Sheol (the place of death and darkness). In the psalms, even *complaining* to and about God is seen as prayer. Psalm 88 laments God's absence, but begins: "O Lord, God of my salvation, when, at night, I cry out in your presence, let my prayer come before you; incline your ear to my cry." Even this most despairing psalm starts by prayerfully invoking God's presence.

Second, although God is present always and everywhere, there was a sense among Jews that we needed to pray *at particular times.* The psalms speak often of praying especially in the morning, in the evening, and at night. Here is the earliest biblical evidence for fixed-hour prayers. Jews practiced daily prayers at set times (Ps. 55:17; Dan. 6:10). We are familiar with how Daniel insisted on keeping fixed-hour prayers, at the risk of being cast into the lions' den. The point is not just that he was pious; but that he felt that this Jewish custom was worth his life.

Temple sacrifices were offered twice daily by Jews, in the morning and evening. As well as praying before meals (another tradition Christians owe to Jews), Jews prayed twice a day, morning and evening, and perhaps a third time, at noon. Each time, they recited a famous text from Deuteronomy 6 (called the *Shema*): "Hear, O Israel: The Lord is our God, the Lord alone. You shall love the Lord your God with all your heart, and with all your soul, and with all your might." Many devout Jews still pray this confession twice a day.

PRAYING MORNING, EVENING, AND NIGHT

Prayer is not my first instinct in the morning. Usually, grogginess, preparing for work, getting kids off to school, and pondering the day's challenges weigh me down and preoccupy me. In the evening, there is always so much I want to get done, or I am just too tired. But fixed-hour prayer keeps calling and inviting me to praise God: here, now, always, and everywhere. The psalms show at least two reasons for praying at particular times.

They confirm that we can know God's presence at all times only if we set aside *certain* times for prayer. The Jews did not buy into a more current notion that since God is present everywhere and in all times we can pray whenever we feel like it. Rather, they believed that praying regularly at set and specific times helps focus and reorient one to God *at all other times*.

The psalms go further by suggesting that at particular moments of the day it is easier to be aware of God.

The psalmist often speaks of praying, worshiping, sacrificing, singing, or complaining to God in the morning. Psalm 59:16 says, "I will sing aloud of your steadfast love *in the morning.*" Or look at Psalm 88:13: "*In the morning* my prayer comes before you." Psalm 5 says, "O Lord, *in the morning* you hear my voice; *in the morning* I plead my case to you, and watch." Suzanne Guthrie translates the first part of this verse this way: "At daybreak you listen for my voice, as if the psalmist is saying that God waits and listens for that first word of prayer before anything else can happen."[1] That translation has a nuance of God paying particular attention in the morning. Traditionally, certain psalms are used in morning prayer: 3, 143, 57.

In the morning God blesses us in special ways, and hence this is an important time to pay attention. In Psalm 30:5, the psalmist says: "Weeping may linger for the night, but joy comes *with the morning*." Even nature plays a part, as we see in Psalm 90:5, where the psalmist writes of "grass that is renewed in the *morning*." Elsewhere, in Psalm 65:8, the psalmist speaks of how morning and evening are special messengers of God: "You make the gateways of the *morning* and the evening shout for joy."

What we bring to a situation affects how we perceive it. Once, people assumed that birds sing because they are praising God. But now we think they are just calling for food or fulfilling some other practical function. In the delightful Celtic legend of Brendan the Navigator, Brendan and his fellow monks went on a long voyage and had many strange and marvelous adventures. On one mysterious island, they encountered a flock of birds that sang psalms at evening and morning prayers and at other hours as well: "Beating their wings against their sides, . . . they continued singing . . . for a whole hour. To the man of God and his companions the rhythm of the melody combined with the sound of their beating wings seemed as sweet and moving as a plaintive song of lament." The monks were awestruck by the birds who "day and night . . . praised the Lord."[2]

I much prefer to believe that birds are praising God, just as I honor the psalmist's ancient idea of morning and evening as gateways that shout for joy. What a gift in our relentlessly busy culture to see certain times as opportunities to perceive or meet God.

In Psalm 90 the psalmist hopes for God to touch us in special ways at this time: "Satisfy us in the *morning* with your steadfast love, so that we may rejoice and be glad all our days." Morning—see Psalm 92:2—is a key time to declare God's steadfast love for us.

No wonder, then, that so much of the traditional emphasis in fixed-hour prayers has been on the importance of the morning.

The psalmist also speaks of evening prayers. The "gateways" verse quoted above reminded us how evenings lend praise to God. The evening, like the morning, the psalmist might say, is a time both of blessing and of hazard. Either way, it is a good idea to pray, whether to praise or to complain and lament. (See 55:17.) Like morning, evening is a key time for prayer according to the psalms, and many psalms lend themselves to evening prayer.

The psalms also make a case for prayer at night. The psalmist mentions night even more than evening as a key prayer time. Consider this famous verse in Psalm 63:5–6: "My mouth praises you with joyful lips when I think of you on my bed, and meditate on you in the watches of the *night*." In the longest psalm

(119:55), he says, "I remember your name *in the night*, O Lord. . . ."

The psalmist sees the night as one of God's messengers: "*Night to night* declares knowledge" in a way that gives glory to God (19:2). Night can be a time of God's protection, too: 78:14; 91:5; 105:39; 121:6; 139:12. God often ministers to us then, says 42:8: "At *night* [God's] song is with me, a prayer to the God of my life."

Such nighttime themes are summed up in a famous psalm, 134:1–2, which is often used for night prayers:

> Come, bless the Lord, all you servants of the Lord, who stand by *night* in the house of the Lord. Lift up your hands in the holy place, and bless the Lord.

Jews said fixed-time prayers two or three times a day. An intriguing psalm suggests more: "*Seven times a day* I praise you for your righteous ordinances" (119:164). We do not find evidence of such frequent prayer being a norm. But on the basis of this verse, monks much later on tried to pray *at least* that often.

The idea of praying in the morning and evening or night—even the substance of such prayers as they developed in the traditions of the liturgy of the hours— is intrinsic to the psalms. We can hardly claim to take the psalms seriously without honoring this tradition too.

"All these were constantly devoting themselves to prayer. . . ." (Acts 1:14a).

"They devoted themselves to the apostles' teaching and fellowship, to the breaking of bread and the prayers." (Acts 2:42). What do we know about prayer in the New Testament, especially as it relates to fixed-hour prayer?

The Gospels show Jesus praying on his own and in synagogues. He also prayed at regular Jewish times: morning (Mk. 1:35) and evening (Mt. 14:23, Mk. 6:46). Perhaps the hymns and psalms that Jesus and the disciples sang at the Last Supper—see Mk. 14:26, Mt. 26:30—were Jewish evening prayers. Jesus, a committed Jew, maintained normal Jewish fixed-hour prayers. He also exceeded them, often praying through the night, for example.

While we have details about *when* Jesus prayed, we find that he taught only one prayer as a model: the "Lord's Prayer," also called the "Our Father."[3] Versions are found in Lk. 11:1–4 and Mt. 6:9–13. In the Luke passage, Jesus taught the prayer in response to the disciples' request, "Lord, teach us to pray, as John taught his disciples." Some see this as a request about *how* to pray. But Joachim Jeremias, the New

Testament scholar, rejects that hypothesis. He argues that they would have known how to pray, but—like other religious groups—wanted their own distinct prayer.[4] He says they wanted "a fixed prayer" and argues that the Lord's Prayer was actually the first Christian Office. In the early centuries of the church it actually was prayed as an Office, two or three times a day by faithful Christians.

The book of Acts is also revealing about early Christian prayer. The disciples prayed together and in the temple and in synagogues, especially at particular times. Here again a careful reading reveals a fixed-hour tradition. This is often overlooked, just like those beautiful birds near my childhood home, or those neglected references to morning, evening, or night prayer in the psalms.

People familiar with the Gospels or the book of Acts (especially older Scripture translations) know that sometimes there are intriguing references to the "third," "sixth," or "ninth" hours. Daytime (however long or short) was divided into twelve hours. The *third* hour was approximately three hours after sunrise, the *sixth* was approximately noon, and the *ninth* was associated with three hours after noon. These hours were announced publicly and were a convenient time to pray. In Scripture, these are the only times specifically and repeatedly associated with prayer.

In the book of Acts, these three hours are connected to prayer. Pentecost happened at the *third hour*, while disciples were together, presumably praying. In Acts 3, Peter and John pray at the *ninth hour*, "the hour of prayer. . . ." Cornelius had his vision—in chapter 10—while "keeping the ninth hour of prayer" (RSV). In Acts 10, Peter has an amazing vision while praying at the *sixth hour*.

This is more than a matter of people deciding to pray at certain convenient times. Some of God's most important actions (Pentecost, the vision of Peter and Cornelius) happened then. At the very least, those times were worth celebrating as mini-anniversaries of God's great work. (Now we might call them small church seasons.) It is interesting too that the Gospel writers closely connected the events of Jesus' suffering with these three key hours. Jesus was crucified in the third hour (Mk. 15:25). There was darkness from the sixth until the ninth hour (Mt. 27:45; Mk. 15:33; Lk. 23:44). Jesus cried out to God and died in the ninth hour (Mt. 27:46; Mk. 15:34).

The Bible was written with too much care and deliberation for this to be coincidence. Scripture writers were not just careful time watchers. Rather the evidence suggests that the third, sixth, and ninth hours had special significance and became important moments for prayer.

Indeed, Christian tradition grew more explicit in recommending prayers in the third, sixth, and ninth hours and tied such prayers to remembering the events of salvation. (Another Church Father, Cyprian, suggested that the three times of prayer—morning, noon, and evening—should be connected to the persons of the Trinity.)

THEMES OF PRAYER FROM THE EARLY LIFE OF THE CHURCH

In the first and second centuries, there were many references to prayer at three fixed times. As time passed, other prayers were added. By the third century, authors referred to prayers as many as five times per day.

Certain themes emerge in early Christian prayer.

First, daily prayer was a high priority from the beginning. Anna, who "never left the temple but worshiped there with fasting and prayer night and day" (Lk. 2:37), may have been a model for this ideal.

Second, prayers were said at certain set times. (Additional prayers were permitted, of course.) Morning and evening were strongly recommended, if not mandated. Such prayers included the Lord's Prayer.

Third, prayers were said both corporately and privately. People prayed together when possible. But even when praying apart, they had a strong sense of praying together nonetheless, since their prayers had similar content and were said at the same time. This is still one of the best reasons for common morning and evening prayer.

Fourth, a persistent New Testament theme was "unceasing prayer" (Mt. 7:7–8; Lk. 11:5–13, 18:1; Col. 4:2; Eph. 6:18; 1 Thess. 1:2; 5:16–18). Some argue that Paul's call to pray "continually" and "without ceasing" is a reminder to the early Christians to observe the hours of prayer. "The command 'Pray constantly' in Romans 12:2 can mean: 'be faithful in observing the rite of prayer.'"[5] (The New Jerusalem Bible translates this as "keep praying regularly.")

So we see that the early centuries of Christian life and the Scriptures themselves provide us with ample reasons to take seriously daily prayer. Unfortunately, this heritage suffered in the following centuries, and it is to that history we now turn.

CHAPTER 4

Where Have All the Hours Gone?

How the Office Was Lost

OFTEN WHEN I SPEAK about fixed-hour prayer, whether in the Mennonite church where I pastored or in seminary classes, people are surprised by this apparently new approach to prayer. The simple truth is that an astounding number of Protestants have never heard of it. Or have heard nothing good about it. When we see how important fixed-hour prayers were to early Christians, this is astonishing.

What happened to make such practices disappear from the radar screen of so many Christians?

THE FOURTH CENTURY

Nowadays, it is often hard to gather people together once a week. But in the fourth century it was normal for most churches to have morning and evening prayer every day. Many participated. Christian leaders expected regular attendance. Ambrose of Milan (339–397) wanted Christians to come at least each morning.

The church was not yet centralized, so the Office varied from place to place. Yet the services had much in common throughout Christendom. They revolved around the psalms, were carefully structured, drew people's involvement by their movement and inviting rituals, and took little time. They were accessible, available, and engaging.

MONKS AND PRAYER

During the fourth century, in Egypt and Syria, some Christians withdrew to the wilderness. These first monks were highly critical of the church and its clergy. They abandoned the world and rejected the church as being too comfortable. This also cut them off from the worship of the wider church.

They longed to fulfill literally Paul's injunction to "pray without ceasing." Morning and evening prayers were not enough. They also saw secular life as a deterrent to prayer. The wilderness afforded fewer distractions. They added prayer offices and so daily spent many hours in prayer. Eventually there were up to eight services, including one in the night. There was even controversy about having fixed-hour prayers, however many there might be. An early monastic, John Cassian (c. 360–430), lamented that set times fell short of unceasing prayer.

Monastic worship was different not only in quantity but also in style from nonmonastic churches. For one thing monks prayed the entire Psalter in order (often every week, though some did so every day). This increased the amount of time spent in worship. More significantly, psalms were no longer for corporate worship but were used essentially for personal edification, reflection, and meditation. They were often followed by silent rumination. Monastic services had more to do with private prayer. Their worship was geared toward individual edification.

Monastics accomplished many great things and continued to do so in many places as missionaries, preservers of scholarship and wisdom, and teachers of prayer. We can be grateful for this movement. But ironically, monastics moved in directions that helped divorce corporate worship from personal spirituality by putting so much emphasis in their services on personal and private reflection.

MONASTICISM GOES TO THE CATHEDRAL

Eventually, some desert monastics moved to cities and towns. Church leaders were happy to have such gifted and committed participants and often invited them into positions of leadership. Gradually, monks shaped worship more and more. Their influence included adding elements to morning and evening services (making them longer) and also additional services. Services also grew more complex to sing.

Gradually, corporate public worship that was once available to all changed to long, inwardly oriented devotional services available to fewer and fewer folks. Ironically, while on the one hand this movement helped encourage fixed-hour prayer, on the other hand its emphases were so burdensome for most people that such prayer became more and more restricted to the religious elite.

Paul Bradshaw, a church historian specializing in worship, spells out contrasts between daily prayer before and after monasticism's influence.[1] For one, worship moved from corporate emphasis to individual prayer. Previously, simple, colorful worship involved the entire congregation, but gradually only priests and monks needed to be present. Lay people did not even need to be there; there was no role for them. Prior worship emphasized praise (via psalms and canticles) and intercession. Monastic worship was subdued and inward looking. Fixed-hour prayers were becoming privately oriented.

The idea of unceasing prayer changed, too. When people gathered twice a day, it meant that their whole lives would be prayerful. But monks saw unceasing prayer as spending as much time as possible in church, ruling out those who were not priests or monks. Yet even with such drastic changes, there was still a strong sense of twice-daily prayer.

Alas, in the Middle Ages the estrangement between corporate worship and personal spirituality deepened. Services grew longer and more complex. There was a gap between Latin and the local language of many people. Involvement grew increasingly difficult for laypersons; most did not understand the services, and the layout of churches made it difficult for them even to see what was happening. Lay participation was not necessary, practically or theologically. "Professionals" conducted services *on behalf of* "lesser" or "secular" Christians.

Eventually each church and priest was expected to observe all eight offices. The demands of reading and praying so much Scripture—possible for monks or clergy—was impossible for others. The complicated observances required many books. Increasing numbers recited the offices privately, even though this was supposed to be discouraged. Yet private recitation was encouraged for mendicant traveling orders (Franciscans, Dominicans). Members of these orders were unable to carry all the prayer manuals and books, so breviaries (one-volume portable Office books) were developed.

Many laypersons moved away from corporate prayer. Wealthy people turned to private observance via beautifully illustrated Books of Hours, *"the medieval bestseller, number one for nearly 250 years.*

More Books of Hours . . . were produced during this period than any other single type of book, including the Bible."[2]

People found alternatives to corporate worship: pilgrimages, *Paternoster* (Lord's Prayer) devotions, Stations of the Cross, veneration of saints, and the rosary. Individual devotions meant that people did not need corporate worship. Often when they attended, they did not participate in the service—neither understanding the Latin nor receiving communion—but just said their private devotions.

Movements such as the fourteenth-century *devotio moderna* (later so influential on many Reformers) emphasized interior and subjective prayer. Corporate worship was being separated from personal devotion.

Daily prayer was no longer available or accessible to the church at large. In effect, it was for those who lived distinct and separate lives in the cloister. The Office was in trouble. Many priests were burdened by the obligation of praying all the daily fixed hours. Some new orders abandoned corporate prayers altogether.

THE REFORMATION AND THE OFFICE

When he was a monk, Luther at times accumulated three weeks' worth of prayers and then recited them without food or water for however many days it took, even when this practice made him physically ill. He gave this up when he fell three months behind. He was frustrated with the Office. There was too much attention on fantastical stories about saints and little attention to Scriptures, so God's word was silenced. And such prayer was done as an obligatory work as if salvation could be earned. Later he tried to maintain a pared-down morning and evening service that involved preaching. But it tended to serve only clergy, seminarians, and academics, and soon fell mostly into disuse. As well, he created "house breviaries," private morning and evening prayers to be conducted at home, alone or with one's family.[3] (This is the ancestor of family devotions, which my parents and grandparents practiced, but it is a tradition that has by now largely disappeared.)

Other Protestants tried to modify fixed-hour prayers. Some—Zwingli, for example—instituted daily services, hoping they would again serve the whole church, not just priests and monastics. The Protestant custom of morning and evening Sunday services is a vestige of the morning and evening Office. Local languages were preferred in worship over Latin. Simpler music was employed. Fewer services were sung. The church calendar was simplified. But, on the whole, Protestant devotions were relegated to pastors' studies, family prayers, or school chapels.

Anglicans *did* retain fixed-hour prayer with *The Book of Common Prayer*, which was heavily informed by monastic tradition. Thomas Cranmer created several versions, collapsing the eight services into two, morning and evening. Apart from Anglican endeavors, though, fixed-hour prayers mostly fared poorly with Reformers. Many people lost even the popular devotions they had had before the Reformation. The abolishing of "monastic hours of prayer, signaled by the church bell, removed the rhythm of frequent times for recollection. What ordinary folk of the Reformation traditions did instead is a relatively unknown story."[4]

The Reformation took to new lengths emphases begun in the late Middle Ages: "a trend to elevate individual, contemplative, and interior prayer as spiritually superior to the communal, external forms of the divine office, which it was thought could present a distraction to 'real' praying." A divorce between personal piety and corporate worship continued to grow until the nineteenth century. With the industrial revolution and urbanization, people lost rural rhythms that permitted regular prayer. Individualism continued to spread, as did a voluntaristic approach to faith. "There were also the effects of the romantic revival and the resurgence of evangelistic fervor. . . ." Growing literacy and mass production of literature also made private devotional material more widely available.[5]

THE ROMAN OFFICE SINCE
THE SIXTEENTH CENTURY

Catholics and Orthodox never lost the fixed-hour tradition. There were reform attempts by Roman Catholics and different breviaries proposed as early as the sixteenth century.

Nevertheless, the Catholic liturgy of the hours was largely private prayer for priests and monastics. Even when laypersons were present, mostly they listened, and often—even during the Eucharist—they said their own private devotions (for example, the Rosary or Stations of the Cross). Thus for much of the past few centuries Rome too reinforced a divorce between private piety and corporate worship.

Important work on the Office was launched by Vatican Two. The liturgy of the hours was revamped. It was pared down to be more accessible to and doable by laypersons. It was to accommodate better many daily lives by focusing on morning and evening prayer as the most important hours of the day. The long Vatican Two process of reforming the liturgy of the hours inspired many scholars of other Christian traditions to look at how the fixed-hour Office can best be applied and practiced again today.

WHERE HAVE ALL THE HOURS GONE?

I am interested in my faith ancestors, Anabaptists (forebears of Mennonites, Amish, and Hutterites). Persecuted by Protestants and Roman Catholics, they had no safe meeting places, so daily corporate prayers were impossible.[6] Yet it seems surprising that they so quickly lost fixed-hour prayer traditions. Many Anabaptist leaders previously had had an Office obligation as they had been priests or monks. Other Anabaptists were exposed to Protestant morning and evening prayers in Zwingli's church. Ironically, Anabaptists did not realize that evening and morning prayer was well established in the early church that they idealized.

Yet our tradition shows vestiges of influences of the Office. (I suspect the same is true for other Protestants.) An early Swiss document says: "The Psalter shall be read daily at home." This was a possible "inheritance from monasticism."[7]

One leader, Balthasar Hubmaier, resumed church bell ringing to call people to common public prayer, overturning previous Protestants who had stopped such a "Catholic" practice. (He did not restore other rejected Catholic rituals.)[8] He justified this call to common prayer by citing the book of Acts and writings by ancient Church Fathers that recommend the third, sixth, and ninth hours of prayer.

In 1534 or 1535 in Halberstadt, Prussia, in a small Anabaptist house church, "The brethren and sisters prayed four times daily, also before and after meals. They usually got up twice at night to pray and praise God." [9] This is a typical time frame for praying the Office.

Hutterites at first abandoned fixed prayers but moved quickly to formal daily prayer, which they still observe. This was easier for them as they lived together. "In 1582 a defector said that in the morning they prayed, 'May God the Father protect me'; at noon, 'May God the Son protect me'; and in the evening, 'May the Holy Ghost protect me.'"[10] Intriguingly, Cyprian (third century) recommended connecting morning, noon, and evening prayers to the three persons of the Trinity.

Anabaptists soon developed prayer books, the first one being for Dutch Mennonites. It included prayers for every day: morning, evening, and before and after meals. Non-Mennonite prayer books were used as sources.[11] Some of their prayer books are still in print.

Halberstadt, Hutterite, and Mennonite prayer books point to a need for formal support in daily prayer. However, although Anabaptists emphasize community, most do not have strong corporate prayer traditions.

It would be interesting to study other Protestant traditions to find vestiges of the Office there. Many family devotions, common even in recent decades, are traces of the Christian instinct for regular fixed-hour prayers.

CAN THE DRIED BONES OF THESE PRAYERS LIVE?

Fixed-hour prayer went from being one of the most important ways that Christians worshiped and prayed to disappearing for most Protestants. Unfortunately, vital understandings of the Office were lost during the time between the early church and the Reformation.

The Reformation responded to real concerns and corruptions. But along the way, much that was worthwhile was lost. This process threw out, among other things, the Office with the holy water, as it were.

Renewing or uncovering the genius of fixed-hour prayer could go a long way to renewing people's prayer and worship life. Common morning and evening prayer could address particular problems in our prayer: what to do, when to pray, avoiding subjectivity and narcissism, connecting with the wider church, and relating to the church year.

How can we move again to taking fixed-hour prayer seriously? One important step will be to understand its theology and purpose. If we know what it *means*, we are more likely able to engage in it again.

CHAPTER 5

Take Our Moments
and Our Days

*A Theology of Morning
and Evening Prayer*

DOROTHEOS OF GAZA, a sixth-century monk in the
Middle East, tells a delightful story about early
morning prayers. An old man "gifted with spiritual
insight" was praying with other monks when he saw
someone "dressed in shining clothes" enter the chapel
carrying a container of oil. At the beginning and ending
of the service, the stranger anointed all the brothers
and even some empty seats. The old man asked this
stranger his identity and the purpose of his actions.
The visitor told him,

> "I am an angel of God, and am ordered to . . . place
> this seal on those found in the church from the
> beginning of the psalmody, and those who remained
> until the dismissal, because of their earnestness and
> zeal and by their own free and deliberate choice."
> And the old man asked, "And why did you sign the
> place of those who were not to be found here?" To

this the holy angel replied, "All those who were zealous and had the generous intention of being there but were absent through some violent sickness and with the abba's blessings, or those who were engaged in fulfilling a command given them under obedience—all these, although absent, received the sign since by their right intentions they were there; but those who were able to be there and through their carelessness were absent, I was commanded not to sign, since they had made themselves unworthy of it."[1]

Although as a pastor I appreciated it when people came to worship on time or even early, I am a little uncomfortable with the righteousness based on works that is implicit in this story. There are other things going on in people's lives that cannot always be overcome even by "earnestness and zeal."

Nevertheless, there is something charming about the image of receiving a blessing while attending worship. We do not just bless God in our praise and worship; we ourselves are blessed. Blessings are seldom only one-way.

More significant, this story reveals how seriously common prayers were once taken. This concept seems foreign now. We have mostly forgotten such ancient traditions. To understand *why* the Office was so important—and still is—it is vital to explore its *theology*.

MORNING AND EVENING

The first thing to note is that such prayer reminds us that morning and evening, the beginning and ending of each day, are not just periods on the clock but are profoundly theological. We saw this in our study of psalms. We also sense a deep spiritual significance in the careful attention to evening and morning in creation in the first chapter of Genesis. Ancient Scripture writers understood that there was something full of potential at these particular times of day.

Is this really so surprising? In the touching novel *Walking Across Egypt*, author Clyde Edgerton writes about the elderly Mattie's morning habits:

It was her favorite time of the day. . . . She also liked it when it was cold and she could stand there taking in the cold morning while the sky was red, and time stopped, stood still, and rested for a minute. People thought that time never stood still, except in Joshua when the sun stood still; but she knew that for a minute before sunrise when the sky began to lighten, showing dark, early clouds, there was often a pause when nothing moved, not even time, and she was always happy to be up . . . in that moment; sometimes she tried to stand perfectly still, to not move with time not moving, and it seemed that if she were not careful she might slip out of this world and into another. That made the moment risky, bright shining, and very still at the same time. She hoped that when her time came, it would be close to morning, and she could wait for the still moment.[2]

What a lovely notion: "Time stopped, stood still, and rested for a minute."

This certainly rings true. We all know "early birds" who preach the benefits of rising early. And when I get up early I am usually grateful. Our experiences, literature, and art all keep reminding us that there is something full, rich, and even holy about sunrises and sunsets. Most people recognize that beauty if they take the time or make the effort to pay attention. Those daily events touch something primal within us. Thus it is not surprising that these two events of the day have often been key moments in different religions through the ages.

Most people have rituals for morning and evening. For some it is juice or coffee in the morning, for others exercise in the morning or evening, or a snack before bedtime. I have heard that Hegel noted that the newspaper replaced morning prayers. Could it be that if we do not dedicate key moments to God that they—like anything that abhors a vacuum—will fill up with something else? How many of us load our day's first or last key moments with the idle chatter of radio deejays or the latest bad, bad news on television?

My father used to watch the news religiously, every evening after supper and before going to bed. He was unhappy about much in the world and the news made him angrier. I am not sure that he learned a lot from this habit or that he could do much about the distant events that angered him.

How are we shaped by our morning and evening habits? Does the raucous humor of early morning deejays edify us? Does hearing the media's daily take on the world's bad news before going to bed help us sleep better? Or does it contribute to deepening despair and anxiety? Christian faith insists that morning and evening are key times for spiritual growth.

The Office keeps drawing and reorienting us to God's perspective. I see my life and my family being held by God and reliably entrusted there. As a pessimist, I find this does not come naturally. But it does free me to remember that as important as any present reality may be, there is a more substantial eternal reality beyond it.

Just as some parents remind us that a hearty breakfast is a requirement for a good day, so wise teachers of spirituality commend the morning, the beginning of our day, as an important moment of prayer, when we set goals and priorities to seek and serve God. Important morning themes include praise, listening, paying attention to God, and commitment. Each morning we commit ourselves to beginning again in

God and paying attention to God's Word and his movement in our life and surroundings.

Every day we receive another chance. A Desert Father, Abba Poemen, said: "Each day is a fresh beginning."[3] But it is not just an opportunity for us. John Cassian said that by dedicating this time to prayer we give God our day's first fruits.[4] Remember, the term "office" is related to offering. Praying at these times makes our whole life a sacrifice of praise, giving glory to God.

Similarly, at day's end we review what happened, see where we met God, confess where we let God down, and relinquish all into God's hands. Important themes of evening prayers include praise, confession, and release to God.

The deep theological nature of evening and morning is spelled out by Eugene Peterson:

The Hebrew evening/morning sequence conditions us to the rhythms of grace. We go to sleep, and God begins [God's] work. As we sleep [God] develops [God's] covenant. We wake and are called out to participate in God's creative action. We respond in faith, in work. But always grace is previous. Grace is primary. We wake into a world we didn't make, into a salvation we didn't earn. Evening: God begins, without our help, [God's] creative day. Morning:

> God calls us to enjoy and share and develop the work
> [God] initiated. Creation and covenant are sheer
> grace and there to greet us every morning.[5]

The way we enter and leave each day is affected by what we do each morning and evening. Our day revolves around these two points. Remember how Psalm 65 says that both morning and evening are special messengers of God: "You make the gateways of the morning and the evening shout for joy."

Evening and morning prayers reflect a central Christian truth, the paschal mystery: Our life comes from the death and resurrection of Jesus Christ. Similarly, we are called to die to our old selves and to sin, and to take up our cross so that we too might know new and eternal life and be born again. Evening prayer is a small death; we surrender ourselves into God's hands. Think of the appropriateness of that classic children's prayer: "If I should die before I wake. . . ." The morning is a small rebirth and resurrection. We often give thanks for a new day and its opportunities. The dying and rising is relived in each daily cycle. Thus, as we observe the morning and evening rhythm, we also have opportunity to live deeply and enter into the most basic and important truths of our faith.

The Office keeps reminding us of God's eternal realities, no matter what. Some time ago, I went to bed discouraged and spent the night sleepless because of some bad news. I got up early the next day for a vigorous bicycle ride in a nearby forest. All was quiet, peaceful, still, and beautiful. The air was clear and cool. In that moment I experienced the refreshment that also often occurs as I pray the Office. Some circumstances were bad, but the world is still a place of much beauty, and God is always to be trusted.

SANCTIFICATION OF TIME

When I asked first Henri Nouwen and later the Abbot who guides me for counsel on living spiritually, both gave good advice. Their first point was this: I need to set apart regular times every day to focus on God and the things of God.

There are basic, mundane things that are nevertheless so vitally important they need to happen every day, every twenty-four hours: brushing and flossing teeth, washing our bodies, exercise, taking vitamins. Spiritual masters teach that prayer is an essential need that must be met at least once a day.

When I visited Christ in the Desert monastery, Br. Isaac, the assistant guestmaster, told me that John Wesley committed five minutes every hour to prayer. (How wonderful that a devout Roman Catholic monk instructed me, a Mennonite, in Methodism.) He also spoke of giving an hour a day and a day a week to God.

Less and less are we exposed to the old tradition of church bells ringing regularly through the day to remind us of God's presence and to call us to prayer. Such reminders sound simple, but can be a surprisingly difficult discipline. I set my computer to chime every fifteen minutes, thinking that could summon me to pray. Even though it was my idea, I find myself incredibly resistant. Yet how much more worshipful and appropriate this is than watches that beep or cell phones that ring during worship services. That beeping is hardly a reverent call to prayer. Rather it just makes us anxious, reminding us that precious time is slipping away.

Praying regularly throughout the day is not always easy, but most spiritual masters urge us to find ways of doing so. (Although morning and evening are key times for this, we also know that careers, life stages, and family situations do not always make this possible.)

Setting aside time daily is related to an important theological idea behind fixed-hour observance, "sanctification of time," making holy both day and night and all that happens during that time.

Sanctification of time urges us to find other ways of looking at and dealing with time. Time can be a place to meet God and to receive God's blessings (like the monastics in Dorotheos's story, perhaps). Meeting God in our lives, in our experience of time, is a good way to speak of the sanctification of time. "Sanctification" means "making holy." Time, which is experienced by many as oppressive, can be turned into divine opportunity by paying attention to God.

Another way to speak of this idea is "redeeming the time" or "making the most of the time," a term from Paul (Eph. 5:16; Col. 4:5). Sanctifying, redeeming, and making the most of time means living in time from God's eternal perspective.

As a pastor, I saw that our experience of time today is a huge spiritual problem. The best of our Christian and Jewish heritage recommends seeing and living in time differently with our prioritizing of daily prayer, weekly sabbaths, religious feasts, church seasons, and sabbatical and Jubilee years. "Christian practices for opening the gift of time resist the inhumane rhythms that shape so much of contemporary life."[6]

The problem is not that time is profane and we try to make it holy. Rather, it is a place where we encounter the holy and where we can be holy, but too often we profane it instead. "Sanctification" literally means "setting apart." In morning and evening prayer, we set apart certain times, hours, and moments to pray, sanctifying them by interrupting regular schedules. In so doing, we resist and even break the tyranny of time, whether it be others' agenda or our own compulsions and misplaced priorities.

It is not only set-apart times, interruptions, that are holy. Rather, we set apart *some* time to pray, pay attention to God, listen to God, and focus on God's priorities, so that *all* of life can be holy. Theologian Heather Murray Elkins has a marvelous term, "altaring time."[7] Her pun suggests *both* the offering of time to God and the fact that that sacrifice *alters*, changes, makes holy our experience of time. We praise God in times of prayer so that we might praise God at all times.

My ancestors in the faith, sixteenth-century Anabaptists, were rightly concerned that too many churches confined God's presence to certain times, places, or people. Our problem today, however, is different. Now there is the real danger that people cannot find God at all in any time, place, or person. Setting aside moments in our day overcomes this challenge.

Offering time is an important sacrifice. It is one of the most precious things we have to give. It is a rare commodity. Giving time, sacrificing and "altaring" it, is an act of worship and praise. Just as giving our money helps us exercise discernment about how we spend money, offering time also helps us exercise discernment about how we spend the rest of our time.

A vital goal of fixed-hour prayer is to make us aware always of God, to be present to God, and to be mindful of God's presence in time, that is, of the "sanctification of time." We begin to live out Paul's ideal of unceasing prayer when our whole lives are lived in the context of our existence in God, when we live faithfully to God, when we bring all our life into our ongoing conversation with God.

Some complain that fixed-hour prayer is boring or repetitive. Not too often does it ignite emotional fireworks, mystical revelations, or ecstatic experiences. But the "ordinariness" of the Office is essential for sanctifying our ordinary lives and for reminding us that God is found in the ordinary and the mundane more than in the extraordinary and the melodramatic. The ordinariness, everydayness, and repetition of the Office help us appreciate God in all of our life, including its humdrum and repetitive rhythms.

Sanctifying time is emphasized at Iona. That's why worship and work are integrated. At the end of the morning service, there is a brief but telling rubric: "We remain standing to leave, the work of our day flowing directly from our worship."

THE OFFICE AS SPIRITUAL ORIENTATION

When I was a pastor, every week I was involved in many different activities. At times these could feel disconnected, but they had something in common. They were intended to help people seek and pay attention to God. As we saw in our reflections on the sanctification of time, we are called to turn toward God in all of our lives and activities.

On Sundays and in daily prayer we test our directions against the direction of God's Reign. We see the need to readjust. Then God's reality and priorities inform us, each day, both in mundane life and in difficult crises. We need ongoing orientation and reorientation in this hard work.

"Orient" originally was a noun meaning "east." The verb was developed for worship: It meant arranging or aligning a church sanctuary to face east. *Orienteering* is a sport of finding one's way through difficult territory or wilderness using only a map or a compass. Both are terms that demand action, not just attitude or attention. It is not enough to turn one's gaze to God: One needs to rework and redirect one's whole life that way. Spiritual orienting calls for people to integrate mind, heart, and hand into the life to which God calls us.

Fixed-hour prayer serves as a major means of orientation: "As the scanning ray of the radar screen shows up objects in regular flashes, the daily prayers regularly flash up a matrix which we put against the world in which we live our daily lives, and this gives us orientation, so that we discover where we are."[8]

The Office is a regular opportunity to be oriented by and to God's true light.

COMMUNION OF SAINTS

When I was twenty, my seventeen-year-old sister died of complications connected to her leukemia. Being cut off from her was unbearable. Yet I felt that she still existed in some way. Sometimes when I prayed, I asked God to greet her.

When I was thirty-four, my father died of cancer at age sixty-three. Soon I had the strong sense that he could see me, that he was looking on approvingly, even as a cheerleader. (The idea of his being a cheerleader is amusing on several counts.)

I was experiencing the communion of saints. All of God's beloved are still held in God's love, present to God, and significantly present to one another and to us. Being mindful of all the faithful people who have preceded us, we are encouraged and heartened to be faithful. As the Scripture says in Hebrews 12:1–2: *"Therefore, since we are surrounded by so great a cloud of witnesses*, let us also lay aside every weight and the sin that clings so closely and let us run with perseverance the race that is set before us. . . ."* The cheerleading metaphor works well here, too.

Common prayer is a vivid experience of the communion of the saints. Earlier, I wrote about being at Christ in the Desert Monastery where suddenly prayers I had prayed in many different contexts, settings, and places were joined into one. That was an experience of the communion of saints.

Prayer brings unexpected, unlikely—and some would say *impossible*—connections. This is illustrated by the story of a friend who was serving a prison sentence. For years, he received cassette tapes of our worship services. At first, he just longed to hear sermons. But along the way, he asked for bulletins and a hymnal so he could follow along with the prayers and hymns too. Because we sent a package once a month, and the prison was slow in delivering packages, he often did not hear the tapes until months later. Even so, this friend—who is not a Mennonite—did not just *listen* to the tapes but sang and prayed along with the congregation . . . months later.

This example shows that the communion of saints operates not only beyond the limits of geography and space, but also beyond boundaries of time. It connects all Christians everywhere who have ever lived. This prisoner prayed *with* our congregation even though chronologically he did not join in until months later. In a real way we were united.

The communion of saints offers a powerful transcendence. An Orthodox Christian, Anatoli Levetin, was imprisoned in the Soviet Union for providing religious education for youth. During his solitary confinement, his daily prayer was the Orthodox Office.

At 8:00 in the morning I would begin walking round my cell, repeating its words to myself. I was then inseparably linked to the whole Christian world. In the Great Litany I would always pray for the Pope and for the Oecumenical Patriarch, as well as for the leaders of my own church. . . . I felt myself standing before the face of the Lord, sensing almost physically his wounded, bleeding body. I would begin praying in my own words, remembering all those near to me, those in prison and those who were free, those still alive and those who had died. More and more names welled up from my memory. . . . The prison walls moved apart and the whole universe became my residence, visible, and invisible, the universe for which that wounded, pierced body offered itself in sacrifice.[9]

Common prayer is composed of prayers that the church has prayed throughout the ages and around the world. They will be prayed until the end of time, and we may even expect to pray them in the kingdom to come. When we pray them, we are joined with the whole communion of saints, present and absent and future, here and gone and still to come.

In an age and culture of individualism gone seriously awry, such common prayer calls us into a broader solidarity, community, and fellowship that helps us live faithfully in God's Reign.

ROLL CALL? ROLE CALL?

Remember how teachers would take attendance or roll call first thing during our elementary-school years? Roll call is partly an administrative function. Our grades in school had some relationship to attendance. It is not just that the authorities need to know who is there but also that the authorities want their pupils to know who is in charge.

God is not a divine schoolmaster who carefully tracks our every move, rewarding good attendance (despite what Dorotheos's angel suggests), intimidating us, and punishing us for being tardy or absent. Christian faith is not about winning or earning salvation by performing externally imposed legalities.

On the other hand, attendance is important. Was it Woody Allen who said that 90 per cent of life is showing up? Being there, being present, remaining faithful to commitments, are all vital. Even if we are sometimes perfunctory in fulfilling our duties, they can still be important. I once read a study of marriages that survived over the years and the *one thing* that they all had in common was not compatibility, communication, or counseling but the fact that the partners kissed each other every morning and night. Nothing was said about how much passion went into those rituals.

Roll call can be a ritual that speaks to us on a deep level. Teachers also used it as a way of slowing us down from the excitement and noise we brought in

71

from before classes. It was a reminder to *us* of *who* we were (students) and *where* (in school). It was a *role* call, having to do with identity and responsibility.

When we pray the Office, praise God, and hear Scriptures and respond to them, we are invited to ponder God's questions, challenges, and call. We are reminded that we are God's beloved children and are called to live out our discipleship to Jesus. In this roll call, we are reminded of God's presence and summoned to pay attention to God's priorities, not just during this prayer but during everything that the day brings.

In the praises we give to God, there are implied questions for us. Are you there? Are you ready? Are you available? Are you willing to work for and promote God's Reign and priorities?

Some of the most challenging Bible verses are questions that cut us to the heart. In Genesis 3:9, God asks Adam: "Where are you?" In Genesis 4:9, Cain tries to evade responsibility by answering God's question with one of his own: "Am I my brother's keeper?" In John 21:15 and following, Jesus asks Peter three times: "Do you love me?" God's challenge to Isaiah also confronts us: "Whom shall I send, and who will go for us?" (Isa. 6:8).

Such questions are there every time we pray and celebrate fixed-hour prayer. In many versions of morning prayer, we hear the psalmist's refrain:

O that today you would listen to [God's] voice.
Do not harden your hearts, as at Meribah,
as on the day at Massah in the wilderness.
(Ps. 95:7b–8)

This is both a challenge and an invitation. We sometimes think that prayer is about influencing God, possibly by our petitions, perhaps by our piety. But here we see that prayer affects, influences, and alters *us* . . . or is that *altars* us?

Some churches toll a bell several times a day. Everyone is invited to stop work and prayerfully remember the angel's words to Mary. This practice is the Angelus, an old medieval tradition created so that regular working folk who could not go to the church's elaborate services could experience a "small Office" and turn to God during the day. The famous Jean François Millet painting of peasants praying in a field with a church in the background beautifully illustrates this practice. One monk sees the Angelus as an important question, a *role* call,

a daily opportunity . . . to consent to God's gift of [God's self] to me, and to say, "Here I am, Lord. . . . I am ready." Repeating Mary's words of acceptance becomes my act of yielding to God's will for me in the present situation. Day after day this custom places me before God in an attitude of total personal surrender. . . ."[10]

We too are invited in such moments of praise and prayer to respond as did Isaiah: "Here am I; send me" (Isa. 6:8), or as did Mary (whose canticle is recited in evening prayer), "Here am I, the servant of the Lord; let it be with me according to your word" (Lk. 1:38).

RESTORING THE MISSING LINK

Christians offer worship to God in three ways: public worship, free private prayer, and common prayer. The Office is a "missing link" between corporate and private prayer. Its absence has led to much distortion for Christians in *both* corporate worship and personal prayer. We need a threefold worship and prayer life. The schism between corporate worship and private prayer can be healed if Christians practice all three.

Praying together at a similar time (even when separated geographically) can profoundly reverse unhealthy individualism in our prayer. Moreover, honoring all three forms of prayer actually means they are united. Our lives—and the various kinds of prayers, on Sundays and during the week—grow into one prayer.

Common prayer can leave room for personal prayer and the Spirit's movement. Linking these elements strengthens private prayer by rooting and grounding it in the wider church's fixed-hour prayer. As we grow in the practice of fixed-hour prayer and devotions, our appreciation for corporate worship is reinforced.

There are several ways that the Office connects to weekly corporate worship, drawing from that worship but also deepening it.

On a continuum from corporate worship to private prayer, fixed-hour prayer falls in the middle. On one end Sunday worship involves a large group, less participation, and much formality. Morning and evening prayer involves smaller groups and is more dependent on voluntary initiative and participation, and while it has a degree of formality there is more room for one's own responses, petitions, and modifications. On the other end, private extemporaneous prayer is individual, informal, subjective, and dependent on one's own initiative, and one's responses and petitions are individual.

Both Sunday worship and fixed-hour prayer follow the same basic threefold structure: praise (psalms, hymns, canticles), listening to God (Scriptures, silence, homily), and responding to God (meditation, prayer, intercessions, commitments, offerings, praise, service, and ministry). Common prayer reiterates themes from Sunday worship and prepares us to worship and sing God's praises with the larger group. The Office is enhanced if what is sung there connects with what is sung on Sunday. People often say that they are better prepared for Sunday worship and more receptive to it when they regularly practice morning and evening prayer. As one parishioner told me, "Sunday worship seems less out of sync with the rest of life."

The Office is a recommitment of primary values that we hear preached and that we proclaim each Sunday. It deepens and reinforces baptismal vows. That is one reason for which it is appropriate to recite great Creeds as part of fixed-hour prayer.

Like Sunday worship, common prayer is meant to be prayed with others. Ideally it should be offered and hosted and encouraged by churches. Thus even when one does have to pray it alone, one can remember the wider group and of course the communion of saints as well.

Another church worship connection is that for many centuries churches rang bells several times a day to call people to pray. Thus fixed-hour prayers were sparked by an audible reminder from the very place where they corporately worshiped.

Daily morning and evening prayer also connects with Sunday worship because certain elements (psalms, Scriptures, responses, intercessions, petitions) change with the liturgical season. For at least half the year, this happens within each month or two. Then the Office helps reinforce awareness of the church year.

Thus, Office disciplines offer much hope and promise in restoring the missing link between personal prayer and corporate worship. Even so, it can be an uphill battle to persuade people of the gifts of fixed-hour prayer.

A particular obstacle in our day is resistance to and suspicion of disciplines and formality in the spiritual life. We put so much emphasis on spontaneous inner experience and personal satisfaction, that it is hard to believe that formal prayers can be worthwhile.

Are there other ways of understanding and looking at disciplines that can help us appreciate fixed-hour prayer?

CHAPTER 6

The Freedom of Disciplines

The Primary Paradox of Prayer

WHEN I GO TO THE MIDDLE EAST I am impressed by the periodic cessation of regular activity while prayers are publicly broadcast over outdoor loudspeakers. Muslims stop, spread prayer blankets, kneel, and pray. Such prayers are not always convenient. My first night in Syria followed two long flights, an arrival around 2:00 A.M., and losing a previous night's sleep. It was not a pleasant surprise to be awakened by publicly broadcast prayers within only a few hours after my arrival. While the prayers disoriented me, I recognized their worshipful quality and was challenged and encouraged by it.

In the West, Muslim prayer and minarets are getting more familiar. In Oslo, Norway, Muslims were granted permission to broadcast prayers from rooftops once on Fridays (their holy day). Until then, the only legal call to prayer was the ringing of church bells. (The Norwegian Heathen Society was upset by this development and applied for and received permission for regular announcements of their meetings and values.)[1]

I heard of some Protestant pastors visiting the Holy Land for the first time. The Muslim prayers offended them. "Lo, how the heathen rage," scoffed one. Praying regularly does not strike me as particularly heathen. We North American Christians seem far more heathen in our *inability*—or is that *refusal?*—to pray regularly. Ironically, there is a strong possibility that Mohammed learned his practice of regular daily prayers from a Christian hermit. If so, Muslims are more faithful than many Protestants in maintaining an ancient Christian tradition.

John Moschos, a sixth-century monk, traveled through the Eastern Byzantine Christian world. One commentator notes: "Certainly if John Moschos were to come back today it is likely that he would find much more that was familiar in the practices of a modern Muslim Sufi than he would with those of, say, a contemporary American Evangelical."[2]

For many Christians, with our Western bias against the East and pejorative caricatures of Muslims, the challenging example of Islam will hardly be a compelling argument to take daily prayers more seriously. More's the pity. We could learn a lot from Muslims about the worth and value of recovering our own ancient and venerable Christian tradition of regular daily prayers.

IS GOD NOT EVERYWHERE AND ALL THE TIME . . . AND ALWAYS THE SAME?

When I teach about morning and evening prayer, I run into some common objections. People say they can pray anywhere at anytime, for God is everywhere and is always available. They remind me of people who used to tell me—when they learned I was a pastor—that they do not go to church on Sundays but prefer to worship God in the woods or on the golf course.

God is everywhere and available to us at all times, but this does not rule out the importance of setting aside special times and places for the worship of God. St. Benedict also declared that God is present everywhere and then adds, intriguingly: "But beyond the least doubt we should believe this to be *especially* true when we celebrate the divine Office."[3]

A little Jewish lad insisted on running off to the woods every day, even though such behavior was forbidden. His parents were baffled, because in all other respects he was devout and obedient. Finally, they turned in desperation for help from their rabbi. He talked with the boy, explaining why he must not run off to the woods anymore. The boy listened attentively but the next day did it again. So the rabbi followed from a distance and witnessed the little fellow piously reciting the *Shema* in the woods.

Afterwards, the rabbi asked him, "Why do you do this? Why do you go to the woods to pray? Is not God everywhere and always the same?"

Without hesitation, the boy responded. "Yes, that is true. God is everywhere and always the same. But I am not."

Since we are not everywhere and always the same, we need special times and places to draw our attention to God again, so that this attention can inform, form, shape, inspire, and orient the rest of our lives (with the hope that we will grow more consistent, authentic, and integrated).

While some may be able to be always and everywhere attentive to God who is in all places at all times, most need more structure than that. I found, both in my own experience and in working with parishioners and ministry students over the years, that prayer goes better when there are regular times to pray.

Similarly, it is easier for most to pray in certain places. When I drive into the parking lot of the monastery where I have been praying, worshiping, and retreating for over twenty years, I can feel the tension automatically draining off my shoulders. My body knows how to pray there and knows what to expect when I am there. (This is all the more remarkable, as I am not usually attuned to my body.)

THE PRIMARY PARADOX OF PRAYER: GRACE AND DISCIPLINE

Prayer—as part of our relationship with God—is a gift. God starts and initiates it, whether we deserve it or not, ask for it or not, pay attention to it or not. There is no indication in the early chapters of Exodus that Moses is looking for, waiting for, longing for, or even particularly interested in God. We do not know whether he was especially observant or faithful. We do know that he was an escaped criminal, a murderer who abandoned his own people and the people who had adopted him. Yet God chose him.

But prayer also needs our response. We cannot finally "keep company with God" (Clement of Alexandria's description of prayer) and grow with God unless we make the effort. Like Moses in Exodus 3, we too must "turn aside and look at this great sight," and when God addresses us, we too must say, "Here I am." While a life of prayer is grace-filled, it also depends on discipline and work.

As I explained earlier, my bird watching began without deliberation. I went for regular walks in a nearby park. One day, a friend lent me a zoom lens, and I was astounded by what I saw. Discovering birds was an accident of grace. They were there all long, just as they had been in my childhood neighborhood all along, but I had not noticed.

But bird watching is not just grace, it is also discipline. It is usually best when you have skills and tools (binoculars, a field guide). You need to practice birding. You need to go where birds are. You need to be quiet and wait. Much of this is like the life and discipline of prayer.

Disciplines guarantee nothing. You may have binoculars and a field guide and go to the woods, marsh, or shore, and still see nothing astounding. You might not see a single bird, let alone an interesting one. But the chances are better with disciplines in place. Prayer is like that; discipline is no guarantee that we will encounter God, but our chances improve.

Seeing birds is paradoxical. There are no guarantees, although discipline often helps. When I visited Costa Rica, I was excited because that is one of the world's best places for bird watching. A friend and I went to a famous rainforest, both hoping to see a rare and lovely Quetzal. Some people went there for days at a time without sighting one. We went for twenty-four hours and saw one three or four times. Partly it was the discipline of being in the right place at the right time and knowing how and where to look and listen. But partly it was also grace and good fortune. We certainly did not "deserve" such a sighting.

Sometimes birding happens by grace, even by accident. I have seen good birds as I drove along and was not looking for them. I once saw an Anhinga, of all things, in a small Michigan lake, even though it was much farther north than usual. Once a wild turkey wandered into our suburban backyard. Boy, was he lost.

But even so, discipline was involved in such moments of grace. And that is because one cannot see what one does not notice. And one does not notice if one is not paying attention. I would not have recognized the birds on the road, in that lake, or in my backyard if I did not have bird-watching disciplines. Like Moses, we all must learn how to "turn aside and look at this great sight."

God's grace is all around and often available, but we seldom notice or know it. A nineteenth-century poem by Elizabeth Barrett Browning sums this up well:

Earth's crammed with heaven,
And every common bush afire with God;
But only he who sees, takes off his shoes.
The rest sit round it and pluck blackberries,
And daub their natural faces unaware. . . .

HOLY HABITS

We sometimes connect discipline with another unappreciated word, "habit." We associate this word with "empty habits" or—far worse—"bad habits" or "nasty habits." While habits, like disciplines, can be meaningless, empty, or nasty, they do not have to be so. Habits can be positive and rich.

As a pastor, I encouraged my congregation to share every week things for which we are grateful. We did this as part of the offering time in our worship. After each named gift, the congregation would respond, "Thanks be to God," preferably with vigor and enthusiasm.

One summer day, our family came home from an all-day outing. Upon our return, my wife discovered that we had not turned off a stove burner. As if this were not bad enough, she also saw that we had left a cloth potholder near that live burner. It could easily have caught fire. Fortunately, it had some flame retardant.

My wife showed this to our son, who was then eleven, and she said, "All I can say is, 'Thanks be to God.'"

"I already did." He responded.

There a habit bore fruit. A learned worship refrain informed their lives and their attitudes, and their reading and interpretation of their circumstances.

Similarly, the fixed-hour prayer habit teaches us words and refrains that not only inform the rest of our life but also help us understand, interpret, and frame whatever happens: "Glory to the Father, and to the Son, and to the Holy Spirit, as it was in the beginning, is now, and will be forever. Amen." "O God, make speed to save us; O Lord, make haste to help us." "O Lord, open our lips; and our mouth shall proclaim your praise." There is no day in our life where these holy phrases are irrelevant. The holy habits of prayer can help make them an intrinsic part of our lives.

THE PARADOXICAL FREEDOM OF DISCIPLINE

We often think of discipline as restrictive or limiting, especially in spirituality. But Richard Foster, an evangelical Quaker and an influential contemporary writer on prayer, has a different understanding. He says it has to do with freedom, appropriateness, and discernment. A person of discipline

> . . . can do what needs to be done when it needs to be done. The disciplined person is the person who can live in the appropriateness of the hour. The extreme ascetic and the glutton have exactly the same problem: they cannot live appropriately; they cannot do what needs to be done when it needs to be done.[4]

A disciplined person understands the "signs of the times" and acts appropriately, being free to do what is necessary in the moment.

Tales from the Desert Fathers and Mothers often deal with paradoxes of asceticism versus grace, joy, and hospitality. Anthony was an important desert patron.

> A hunter in the desert saw Abba Anthony enjoying himself with the brethren and he was shocked.

Wanting to show [the hunter] that it was necessary sometimes to meet the needs of the brethren, the old man said to him, "Put an arrow in your bow and shoot it." So he did. The old man then said, "Shoot another," and he did so. Then the old man said, "Shoot yet again," and the hunter replied, "If I bend my bow so much I will break it." Then the old man said to him, "It is the same with the work of God. If we stretch the brethren beyond measure they will soon break. Sometimes it is necessary to come down to meet their needs." When he heard these words, the hunter was pierced by compunction, and greatly edified by the old man, he went away. As for the brethren, they went home strengthened.[5]

Anthony was free to do the right thing at the appropriate time, a freedom he learned because he was in fact a man of tremendous and faithful discipline.

Discipline is freedom to perform beyond original limitations, in ways that are free and liberating. Discipline is neither total restriction nor absolute license. Discipline helps us understand and do what is appropriate; it develops our responses and reactions, enabling us to live according to our priorities.

Our muscles have memory, and that memory is nurtured and built up through practice and repetition. When I was learning to windsurf, I fell into the water a lot. Whether it was due to bug bites, boat wakes, shifts in the wind, muscle spasms, lack of attention, or poor balance, it did not take much to dunk me. But I'll never forget the surprise when one day I went to the lake, got on my board, sailed across the lake with no trouble, and sailed right back again. Yet I had trouble telling my friends how to do this. How could I explain something that had never happened before? My body had learned things through practice. In the same way, our hearts, minds, and souls are conditioned for faithfulness through the deliberate and even at times repetitive disciplines of prayer.

More than that, some things become easier as one masters a discipline. When I began windsurfing, one of the hardest jobs was lifting the mast and sail out of the water. As a beginner, I often dropped the mast while sailing and thus repeatedly had to raise it. But as I practiced more and more, not only did my arms, legs, and back grow stronger for the lifting, ironically I hardly ever dropped the mast, so I did not need to lift it as often. Because discipline made me better, everything was easier.

CHICKADEES AND DISCIPLINES OF GRACE

Some years ago, on a cold winter day, our daughter Erin (then age ten) came home quite excited. Her class had gone on a field trip to a nearby nature reserve. There they had learned to feed wild chickadees by hand.

She told us that she had had no fewer than twenty-nine chickadees sit on and eat from her palm. Our daughter is a nature lover and was euphoric with this experience. We were all in awe, not having experienced anything similar ourselves. We talked to her about St. Francis and his ability to relate to wild animals.

With evangelistic zeal, Erin did not rest content until we too experienced this wonder. She began an impressive lobbying campaign to get us to go soon to the nature reserve. We agreed without too much persuasion.

The designated day for our trip was bitterly cold, one of the iciest of an especially fierce winter. Even before we left, and again in the car, Erin began offering advice and tips on the art—or discipline—of feeding chickadees from one's hand: how to hold one's arm and palm, remaining perfectly still, standing near trees, making certain noises, not fearing or being startled by the little creatures, and not worrying about whether their claws would hurt. As Erin's excitement increased, so did ours.

Carrying our bag of seeds, we made our way across a field, fighting the bitter wind, and came to a sheltered grove. We found places among the trees, assumed the posture Erin recommended, and acted like statues with palms upturned.

All was peaceful. We heard the wind, but here it did not cut so sharply. The trees were snow-laden and lovely. We could see no one else. Gradually, chickadees came into our grove and even more gradually they took the plunge of visiting our uplifted palms.

When one hopped onto my hand, I hardly dared breathe. It was so small and fragile that I could not even feel its weight. (It was so cold that I was not barehanded, alas.) I marveled at how vulnerable the little creature was and wondered at its intricate beauty.

After we had all been visited many times by the small birds, we reluctantly gave in to the cold and trudged away. We all agreed that the words "magical" and even "miraculous" were not overstated. It was a moment of holy, contemplative silence such as one seldom experiences.

It was fully possible that we could have stood in that grove for hours rather than twenty minutes and not had one chickadee approach. We could have seen the value and worth of our time there as completely dependent on how "successful" we were. If no birds came, we could have stomped away in disgust and disillusion. But that would be to miss the point.

Our time in the woods was one of availability. We were open to *whatever* might happen or appear. We could do the right disciplines—as Erin instructed us— but could not guarantee the outcome. In the same way, when we pray we make ourselves available to God but do not demand that God make us fruitful, effective, or better.

And this was an experience of communion with ourselves, with each other, with nature, and with God. We were all awed by it. We drank in the beauty and marveled at it. In the same way, prayer is a time for deeper communion.

Ultimately, our prayers and disciplines are not for any purpose except that of deepening our relationship with God and our availability to God, the relationship that is at the heart of our lives' meaning and that transforms all our other relationships.

Discipline, then, frees and enriches us in many significant ways. But the particular discipline of fixed-hour prayer can offer other challenges and difficulties.

CHAPTER 7

Wrestling for a Blessing

Challenges of Morning and Evening Prayer

JOHN HOWARD GRIFFIN IS KNOWN for his classic book, *Black Like Me*, which helped expose the horrors and ugliness of racism. He darkened his skin with dyes and chemicals to experience in a small way what others endured nonstop. His book received acclaim, but many in the South where he lived hated him and threatened him at times with death, even in his own town. Many do not know that he was motivated for such risky action by deep Christian faith. Much else about this remarkable man is also overlooked.

While Griffin was serving in the military in the South Pacific during World War Two, an explosion totally blinded him. He nevertheless managed to go on and do many things, including writing two novels, marrying, and raising children. Then in the late 1950s, something miraculous happened. His sight returned unexpectedly. For the first time he was able to see his wife and children. Most of us can hardly imagine how precious that must have been.

One of the greatest gifts—in his words, the "full reason and justification for seeing again"—was the fact that he was able to pray the divine hours again. He called such common prayer "the soul's nourishment, the soul's normalcy, sinking beyond the words to their innermost meaning, seeking and thirsting for it."[1]

Most of us would not regard the ability to pray the liturgy of the hours as a primary benefit of recovering our sight. And Griffin used a lengthy prayer book that would be unwieldy and impractical for most laypersons.

The challenges of praying the Office today are in no way comparable to the difficulties that Griffin faced. Nevertheless we must be honest that this is not an easy practice. And we must frankly examine the challenges.

I once visited a novice monk whose primary work was in the infirmary. He said he loved his annual hermitage retreat because then he did "not have to go to the office." I was confused because he had no desk job. But he was referring to the Office, to daily worship. Perhaps it was no surprise that although there was much that he loved about the monastic life, he did not complete his novitiate.

I love the image of wrestling for a blessing. Jacob faced an unknown foe in his nighttime wrestling match. He received a paradoxical blessing and was also wounded in the process. Fixed-hour prayer is not easy, yet we can fully expect that even and perhaps especially there God can touch and bless us.

BUT IS IT PERSONALLY MEANINGFUL?

From time to time, people tell me they would pray the hours only if doing so were "personally meaningful" at a particular time in their life. While I know such prayer is not for everyone, this subjective approach is troubling.

This approach plays into the individualism of so much personal spirituality, especially since the Reformation. While Christians are called to be community oriented—"For where two or three are gathered in my name, I am there among them" (Mt. 18:20)—we are afflicted by individualism.

Should we be willing to do things that do not feel meaningful if we know them to be good for the Body of Christ? When I worked with a church group to pray fixed-hour prayers during the Easter season, it was striking that this was so helpful to some, including ones who had not prayed for a long time, if ever. Several had never been able to maintain a prayer discipline. One participant with a strong devotional life talked about how hard this prayer was. I asked whether it helped to see her participation as supporting "weaker" members. This made sense to her. The "strong" might take on certain disciplines for the sake of the "weak."

I question whether we always know what we most need and whether that need always feels meaningful. I do not always feel like flossing my teeth. When my children were small, I did not always feel like changing their diapers. I do not always feel like listening to people who are sad or, worse, angry. When I worked on university and seminary degrees, the various requirements did not always feel "personally meaningful." What does this phrase mean? Does it mean we have to *understand* why we are doing this? Does it have to feel good to us before we do it?

We may be overly dependent on emotions. Dietrich Bonhoeffer warned about prayer being "governed by moods which have nothing to do with the spiritual life."[2] Feelings in our spiritual lives go through many transitions. We may not know how to pray (or feel like praying) when we do not feel God's presence. Yet the divine hours provide *regularity in prayer*.

Praying neither "comes naturally" nor makes intuitive sense: "Our lives are bent toward God in a way that is not of our natural inclination. . . ." This is important "in a society that worships individual autonomy, freedom, and detachment, a culture that has taught us to live so that we are determined by no tradition, that we are accountable to nothing outside the self." We must question whether "personal choice is the highest human virtue."[3] Praying according to personal feeling or inclination "is more to seek consolation than to risk conversion. To pray only when it suits us is to want God on our terms."[4]

Prayer is about repentance and conversion. Too often our prayer does not pay attention to God but to our concerns, needs, and priorities. Praying means moving beyond what is personally meaningful now and allowing our agenda to be shaped by something— or, better, Someone—beyond us.

One pretty summer day, I decided to say my prayers outside. I was struggling with feeling let down by a friend. I found a private corner in my backyard. To my surprise, this very friend was working on a house down the block. Had he peeked over the fence he could have seen me praying.

The psalm of the day happened to be 55. I immediately resonated with it: "I am distraught by the noise of the enemy. . . ." I could literally hear my friend's hammering a few doors down.

> It is not enemies who taunt me—I could bear
> that;
> it is not adversaries who deal insolently with
> me—I could hide from them.
> But it is you, my equal, my companion, my
> familiar friend. . . .

I could relate. Often in the midst of prayer I start to surface and recognize my resentments of others and even my vengeful thoughts.

The psalm continues. Two phrases that caught me were these: "But I call upon God, and the Lord will save me" and "Cast your burden on the Lord, and

[God] will sustain you. . . ." This reminded me to trust in and rely on God even when I find others unreliable. When I finished praying that day I knew what I had to do. I walked down the block to see my friend and said, "We need to talk." That was the first step toward reconciliation.

Had I chosen a psalm I *wanted* to pray that day, a psalm that suited my particular mood of being betrayed, it would not have been the fifty-fifth. It might not have seemed personally fulfilling. But that prayer converted me. Choosing to pray "imposed" prayers is often called *objective* prayer because we do it regardless of personal feelings and preferences.

CHALLENGES OF REPETITION

One objection to fixed-hour prayer is repetition. Many resent sameness, whether in daily prayers or Sunday worship, and long for things to be innovative and new. But repetition has virtues. It gives us an accumulated store of knowledge upon which to draw, preparing us to receive new insights.

We are not always ready or able to hear a particular Scripture. But if we repeatedly ponder Scriptures, they can be near our hearts, form our lives, and speak to us when we are ready. It is important to do this vital preparatory work in an ongoing way so that if there are times of crisis the texts and their meanings will be available to us.

Repetition convinces and converts us. Hearing something once may not be enough for us to hear, learn, or understand. That is why advertisers are so repetitive. Similar dynamics are at work in the spiritual life. This reminds me of a Desert Father story:

> Abba Poemen said: The nature of water is yielding, and that of a stone is hard. Yet if you hang a bottle filled with water above the stone so that the water drips drop by drop, it will wear a hole in the stone. In the same way the word of God is tender, and our heart is hard. So when people hear the word of God frequently, their hearts are opened to the fear of God.[5]

We often resist the challenge of Scriptures and need to hear them over and over precisely because of that resistance.

There are things we do not get, understand, or absorb with one or two readings. We need to hear them again and again. Perhaps we dislike repetition because it forces us to plumb deeper, and we may dislike hearing over and over again words that challenge us and make us uncomfortable.

> It's a bit like turning a drill. It might appear boring, but the more you are turning the deeper you get. It's literally boring. But if you only turn it once you don't get very far.[6]

Fixed-hour prayer immerses us in Scriptures. Repetition deepens the meaning of the texts, and helps us to live and understand them more fully.

Once, Henri Nouwen guided me on a retreat for five days. His method was simple. Each day he gave me a familiar Gospel text—the annunciation to Mary, Zechariah's canticle—and asked me to ponder that all day long and then speak to him about it at the end of the day. I knew all the texts well. But I dutifully sat with them, reading and repeating them many, many times for an hour at a time. And I saw things I had never seen before. Some of the verses still speak freshly to me now, on the basis of things I discovered at that retreat. Such are the merits and benefits of repetition.

YIELDING TO GOD IN WORSHIP

Common morning and evening hours can be a difficult form of prayer. Perhaps this should not surprise us as even the term "office" itself carries the suggestion of responsibility and duty.

One helpful way of praying this is to *yield* to it. My temptation is to take in and analyze every word. But there is too much to absorb at every sitting. I need to be immersed in it again and again.

Sometimes I visit a Coptic Orthodox church for Sunday worship. There are many things that I love about being there. The three-hour liturgy astounds me and—even more astonishing—a good part of that service every week *is the very same.* Some Scriptures and the short sermon change. But many prayers and hymns recur each time. Obviously my Coptic friends do not suffer from the Western malady of a low boredom threshold.

As I worship there, listening to the music, smelling incense, hearing many prayers in languages that I do not understand, something happens within. At some point, I surrender to the movement of the worship. "I believe," I cry out in my heart. I allow myself to be carried along on the waves of that service. Similar things happen in charismatic worship.

Fixed-hour prayer functions this way too. It works on us time after time, again and again, sweeping us into worship and into God's purposes if we will only yield to it. This can never happen if we cling to skeptical "been there, done that" attitudes.

FINDING GOD IN THE BORING ORDINARY

Often we expect to be entertained in worship, prayers, and spiritual life. This demand for entertainment is a major factor in so-called "worship war" controversies. Wanting to be entertained all the time is immature. Children's complaints of being "bored" often have to do with their own limitations, often acquired limitations. When they were small they had no trouble being fascinated in all manner of circumstances.

Some duties and responsibilities do feel boring at times. Much of life consists of repeating the same things day after day. They are ordinary and repetitive, but necessary. This is in fact an important aspect of the Office. It helps us see the holy in the mundane. Meeting—or at least waiting for—God in the midst of boredom helps us realize the holy in the ordinary. Just as God is available even in the repetition of disciplined prayer, so God is present in life's humdrums. God is not only present in the ecstatic, euphoric, or extraordinary. All time is sacred, hence the "sanctification of time."

Read spiritual masters. No matter how well or how euphoric our prayer goes for a time—especially in the early days—sooner or later we "hit a wall." Whether it is "desolation" or "dark night," the solution is not to give up on prayer at that point and try something else. Rather, spiritual growth requires one to endure and move through that particular wilderness. Showing up and hanging in there are important. The Rule of Taizé acknowledges that sometimes, faithful common prayer observance is not only not heartfelt but is difficult: "There will be days when the Office is a burden to you. On such occasions know how to offer your body, since your presence itself already signifies your desire, momentarily unrealizable, to praise your Lord."[7] Simple persistent faithfulness is important. Brother Émile of Taizé told me, "No matter how beautiful a prayer is, there's always going to be a need for perseverance, for commitment, and for being faithful. There will be times when we don't feel the beauty. Then we pray the question rather than what we feel."

The hope is that one does eventually move beyond the rote, automatic, or mechanical. But this may be possible only after facing one's problems and limitations in the self-awareness that emerges in boredom. In other words, boredom might be important for self-knowledge. Once when I was complaining about a situation in my spiritual life, a wise guide counseled me, "Go deeper." My urge was to flee, to move on, to go elsewhere. But this person helped me see that the problem of boredom was not with just my own circumstances but also with how I functioned in them. The uncomfortable situation was calling for my growth.

MOVING BEYOND MONOTONY

I am not arguing for rote and boring prayer. Learning to pray the liturgy of the hours, with all its challenges, is meant to lead us into prayer, in the same way that learning scales helps us learn to play musical instruments.

While it often feels like the Office is "all the same," there is much variety. Psalms and Scripture readings change every day. Prayers, readings, responses to Scriptures change with various church seasons, and some elements are new each week. If that is not enough variety, we have choices to make within the prayers:

how long to spend in silence, selecting hymns to sing, subjects for intercession.

Common prayer is a long-term commitment that parallels

> human experiences: an exclusive sexual relationship over a long time; practice of an art or a skill to mastery; raising a child or mentoring a young person. All these require a daily, or near daily, commitment. All involve periods of . . . monotony as well as occasional periods of disruptive challenge. All can eventuate in joy.[8]

OFFERINGS THAT COST US NOTHING?

There is at least one other major reason why we sometimes avoid or resist the discipline of this intense prayer. Norman Shanks, leader of the Iona Community, spoke to me at length about common prayer. While there are many current cultural obstacles to such observance, the truth is that this kind of prayer exposes us to the gospel and radically challenges us. Shanks said, "If one takes the actual words quite seriously some of it's quite hard. The God reflected is a God whose love is compassionate and steadfast but also is tough."

This God does not let us off easily. We are drawn into the way of the cross, a demanding and tough route. That is why it is important that we not be in charge of selecting our Bible texts each day. It is too easy to choose ones that always comfort or console, and consistently reinforce and agree with our point of view. Biblical faith requires us to be vulnerable to challenges, to accountability, to repentance, and to a change of heart. This is absolutely essential if we are to grow in our faith.

This is a difficulty for which I do not apologize. I agree with Gandhi, who said that one social sin is "worship without sacrifice." We cannot offer praise to God without being substantially altered and reworked.

Thus it is no surprise that the members of the Iona Community—in their morning prayers—boldly declare: "We will not offer to God offerings that cost us nothing."

But, paradoxically, such offerings also return great gifts to us.

CHAPTER 8

Giving at the Office

Blessings and Benefits of Morning and Evening Prayer

J. NELSON KRAYBILL, a New Testament scholar and author, is also the president of the Mennonite seminary where I teach. He is an enthusiastic proponent of praying the hours, and we often compare notes about this way of praying.

Recently, he got onto a plane and politely engaged the person beside him. "I really took notice, though, when during the flight the young man pulled out the Roman Catholic liturgy of the hours. The young man explained that he was in seminary preparing for the priesthood, and he invited me to join him for prayers.

"It seemed wise not to sing the hymns aloud in a cabin full of other travelers," Kraybill told me with a laugh, "but we read aloud the antiphonal liturgy and spoke prayers of blessing for each other's ministry. At 30,000 feet, two strangers recognized each other as brothers in Christ sharing a journey. More than anything that happened in our exchange, it was that shared prayer that established common ground and bridged denominational differences between us."

This reminds us of the many gifts of this way of praying. To say "I gave at the office" is a way to avoid further commitment, because we allegedly did our duty elsewhere. But faithful Office observance also gives to *us*.

There are many benefits in such prayer. This is not to suggest seeing prayer as a commodity, using it for what we can get from or out of it. But we do want to celebrate what it offers. Fixed-hour prayer is not necessarily an onerous or empty duty (although some have made it into one) but a tremendous opportunity.

My conviction is that the intrinsic benefits and purposes of such prayer far outweigh the difficulties.

THE GIFT OF WORDS

The primary gift of the Office is quite simple: It gives us words to pray. Some might dismiss this. They say that the best prayers are spontaneous and thus authentic. Richard Foster, an evangelical Quaker, tried to live without liturgy and could not because "regular patterns . . . are, in fact, God-ordained means of grace." After all, he adds, "the Bible is full of rituals, liturgies, and ceremonies of all kinds."[1] We may value extemporaneous over set prayers, yet God continues to speak and has spoken for years through the "fixed" language of Scriptures.

Many do not have the words with which to approach God. They do not know how to pray, dare not pray, do not think their prayers are worthwhile, or even have not a clue what to say to God.

I once gathered in my church a group of people who committed themselves to morning and evening prayers for the Easter season. This was new to most, and none had taken on such a discipline before. Several commented on how much they appreciated being given words to pray and ponder. Such prayer "covers it all efficiently," said one, and added, "I don't have to be worried that I've missed something." She no longer fretted about whether her prayer was sufficient, appropriate, or balanced. She discovered freedom and release. Another participant, who was suspicious of things liturgical, said she was surprised "by how much I liked it. I didn't think I'd respond to someone else's words."

Foster argues that liturgical formula has many benefits. It "helps us articulate the yearnings of the heart that cry for expression" and sometimes "prime the pump" to say more. Liturgy brings us into unity and communion with other Christians who pray these prayers. Religious formulas resist "the temptation to be spectacular and entertaining." Formalized language reminds us that prayer calls us to engage the world on God's behalf and is not just privatized faith. It also helps us avoid the familiarity that breeds contempt. The intimacy of prayer must be always counter-balanced by the infinite distance of creature to Creator. In the Bible it is common for those who encounter God to fall on their face as though dead. The stateliness and formality of the liturgy help us realize that we are in the presence of *real* Royalty.[2]

While God is our friend and intimate companion, God is not our buddy or our companionable teddy bear. The English language is not always good at conveying awe and transcendence. In many languages, French or German or Dutch for example, one is careful about whom one addresses casually. In prayer and worship, there is a case to be made for using language that is beautiful and eloquent.

Mark Galli, an editor at *Christianity Today*, tells how hard it was for him as a pastor for ten years "to come up with fresh, creative, relevant prayers each week for worship. I found my compositions increasingly vapid." Much later, he interviewed Kathleen Norris and came to new understandings. She was concerned about language that does not do justice to mystery. Church language, she said, should not be that of the market or the media, the workplace, or the television.

We could have good discussions about what it means to use culturally meaningful language, but Norris is also surely right in this:

The church needs to give people "memorable speech" (as one poet put it). The Scriptures provide that royally. There's all sorts of memorable speech in the Psalms and the Gospels.[3]

THE GIFT OF WORDS FOR TOUGH TIMES

Earlier, I shared how after my sister's death I lost the ability or desire to pray, a Taizé prayer book helped. Many people have similar experiences. An evangelical lost the ability to pray during a serious depression, but then found the *Book of Common Prayer*: "It was like being winched slowly out of a pit," he writes.[4]

In the Easter season prayer group in my congregation, one person struggled for a long time with a family tragedy. She told us often that it was our common prayer that enabled her to pray for the first time in years.

Learned prayers—even rote prayers—can do this. A parishioner told me that when he was on the operating room table he felt unable to pray . . . until he remembered the Lord's Prayer. Another had just had yet another discouraging visit with her young adult son. She was overcome with tears and unable to pray . . . until she recalled the words of confession that her congregation repeated every Sunday.

It is little surprise then that one fine new Office is *For Those We Love But See No Longer: Daily Offices for Times of Grief* by Lisa Belcher Hamilton. She maintains that such prayer, in the midst of one's grief, does several things. It gives "a nourishing structure in difficult days and clears the way for a more honest knowledge of God, yourself, and your relationships with God and your loved one." It also "offers us a larger purpose than learning to live with our own pain."[5]

A good friend, Anna, began praying this way, using the *New Zealand Prayer Book* (an Anglican prayer book) with her husband after he was operated on for a cancer that proved to be terminal. Married for twenty-seven years, they had never practiced such a discipline. It was important for how they spent their final year together, especially in giving thanks for each day. Anna continues to pray this regularly and finds "consolation in hard times and thankfulness in good times."

Morning and evening prayer is a gift in difficult times and transitions. It is also a gift when we have trouble with God and our relationship with God. As David Adam told me:

If you come across a dry time in your life or a down time, you've actually got this resource [i.e., common prayer] . . . which you can call on, even if you may have to say it quite coolly. You can still say it. I compare it to my wife's cooking. Even when she's not that fond of me, she still cooks for me.

SCHOOL OF PRAYER

A primary benefit of the Office is that it *teaches* us to pray.

Do we learn to pray? Is such prayer sincere? In our most important relationships we *do* need to learn how to talk and communicate. A baby's murmurings and gurglings are delightful, to be sure, but we also teach babies how to speak and are happy when they utter their first words. (Early on, I made lists of the first words spoken by our children.) A baby's spontaneity may change as he or she learns words, but the words help the child communicate so that exchanges are no longer confined to matters of food, warmth, discomfort, and the bathroom, as important as all those are.

While some of the best things I may say to children, to my spouse, or to friends, are spontaneous, I also have to learn *how* to communicate. I am still learning how to speak with my wife, even though we have been married for well over two decades. Learning to communicate never comes to an end.

Just because I acquire wisdom about expressing affection or speaking in the midst of conflict does not mean those communications are not sincere, true, or authentic. That learning helps me communicate better. In the same way, we all need to grow in how to speak to and with God. *Learned* language is important. Many of the spiritual classics through the centuries were written by people formed by and immersed in fixed-hour prayer.

The Office is a *school* of prayer. As we saw earlier, it teaches us actual words, phrases, and prayers with which to pray. Earlier we reflected on holy habits and on how learned prayers became an automatic part of people's spiritual repertoire. This also argues for memorizing certain regular prayers so the words can emerge when we need them. These holy habits school us.

When the disciples wanted to learn how to pray and asked Jesus for help, he taught them the Lord's Prayer, a formulaic prayer that was the *first* Office.

The importance of rote and even memorized prayers can be seen in a surprising way in the little book of Jonah. When Jonah was cast into the sea and was swallowed by a whale, he prayed, but not spontaneously. Instead, he uttered psalms, texts he may have learned in the daily prayers of his faith community. In a moment of crisis and need he relied on the prayers and prayer forms of his faith tradition. Eugene Peterson comments: "This is amazing. Prayer, which we often suppose is truest when most spontaneous—the raw expression of our human condition without contrivance or artifice—shows up in Jonah when he is in the rawest condition imaginable as *learned*.[6] Thus it should not surprise us that even Jesus on the cross, in one of his most heartrending moments, quoted the psalms when

he cried out, "My God, my God, why have you for-
saken me?" (Mk. 15:34b; cf. Ps. 22:1). Learned
prayers, then, are important. This idea is different
from

> the prevailing climate of prayer. Our culture presents
> us with forms of prayer that are mostly self-expres-
> sion—pouring ourselves out before God or lifting our
> gratitude to God as we feel the need and have the
> occasion. Such prayer is dominated by a sense of self.
> But prayer, mature prayer, is dominated by a sense of
> God. Prayer rescues us from a preoccupation with
> ourselves and pulls us into adoration of and pilgrimage
> to God.[7]

Learned prayers and memorized texts do more
than give words to say and pray. They teach us prayer's
deep rhythms and meanings. Some prayers may be
beyond our comfort level: confessing sins or praying
for our enemies, for example. They lead us to forms
of prayer that might not occur to us: praise and
thankfulness. They remind us of God's priorities. In so
doing they teach and form us.

IMMERSION IN SCRIPTURE

Seeing the Office as a school of prayer, we are
reminded that another key gift is the fact that the texts
and words of the Office immerse us in Scripture. It is

not just that the Office encourages us to read, ponder, and meditate on Scriptures every day: Psalms, Old Testament readings, biblical canticles, the Gospels. More than that, many—in fact most—of the prayers and responses are derived directly from the Bible. Most of the *Book of Common Prayer* consists of biblical citations.

Along the way, the Bible was treated more and more individualistically, something to read in private devotions. While personal reading is good, that is too limited for the Bible's sole purpose. It is a worship book, written for corporate worship. In it are prayers and hymns, stories for challenge and inspiration, confessions of faith, letters of consolation and edification, all meant to be shared in worship.

The Office's immersing us in Scriptures familiarizes us with many important Bible texts and themes. Bible readings and prayers may pique curiosity and encourage further study. As such prayer steeps us in the Bible we are formed by biblical faith.

St. Paul said: "Let the word of Christ, in all its richness, find a home with you" (Colossians 3:16). As we pray the Office day after day, meditating on the word of God, the thought forms and truths of that word take hold of us. Our minds are transformed so that we can discern what is the will of God, "what is good, acceptable, and mature" (Rom. 12:12). The

Scriptures begin to soak into our minds and hearts and become part of us. The way we are living is constantly brought into the light of God's word, to be guided and transformed. In particular, the Scriptures expounding the mystery of the birth, death, and resurrection of our Lord Jesus and of the gift of his Spirit come to determine our thinking and our way of life.[8]

TIMELY GIFTS OF THE OFFICE

Our culture has many obstacles to prayerfulness. One is overwhelming "busyness." In my last church, parishioners often complained of being too busy and asked the Elders to address this issue as a number one priority. Ironically, the Elders did not do so for two years because they could not find the time. Increased busyness is not just imagined. From 1969 to 1987, the average person's annual work time increased a full month per year.[9]

As most of us no longer live close to rural rhythms, and as technology helps us overcome darkness, we no longer limit activities to daylight. While this expands opportunities, it also leads to confusion. We can now shop, work, be entertained, or be reached around the clock, all week long—or "24/7," as some now say.

Fixed-hour prayer moves us into deeper ways of understanding and—perhaps more important—experiencing time. A life of prayer means making a fundamental priority and commitment, or our busy culture will decide for us. Fixed-hour prayer helps our commitment in a number of ways.

The problem of dealing with time is so large that it cannot be overcome individually. We need companions who accompany us in trying to live a different way. In common prayer we enter and end each day in God's rhythms and never do so alone. As other Christians accompany us, we also are encouraged to live differently within time.

A problem is that many experience time as random. But Christians are encouraged to be deliberate in approaching time. We mark time by the Christian calendar. On a daily basis, we are immersed in morning and evening prayer rhythms. Fixed-hour prayer enriches time by purposefully shaping and structuring it by God's priorities and perspectives.

In the face of overwhelming demands, options, pressures, and opportunities, it often becomes difficult to know what to do when. All of us need routines where we do not have to (or do not want to) decide what to do next. By committing ourselves to morning and evening prayer, we choose a key practice at those times. The way I originally learned to pray meant that my devotions depended on my ability, schedule, and motivation. Plus I had many decisions—when to pray, what to pray about, which Scriptures to read. The Office frees us from such stress.

Fixed-hour prayer is ideal for busy people. Various versions can easily be prayed in ten to twenty minutes each morning and evening. No matter how busy we are, almost everyone can afford that much time.

A little discipline, practiced faithfully, can in the long run make a vast difference in changing one's life. Esther Quinlan is an American Muslim convert who writes about the joys of observing Muslim fixed-hour prayer (*salat* in Arabic). She writes honestly of how hard it was to learn this discipline. Learning and growth were gradual but ultimately fruitful. "If we set sail from New York, a tack of only five degrees can make the difference between landing in England or Africa. So it is with the *salat*: the smallest effort acts as a tack, and gradually over a long period of time, the effort brings one to the intended destination."[10]

Common prayer changes our experience of time, so we no longer feel harried, controlled, and pressured, but can live in the rhythms of God's grace.

ECUMENICAL GIFTS

An important benefit of the Office is its ecumenical nature. Not only does it join us in the prayers of Christians through the centuries (the communion of saints), but with Christians around the world. While it is difficult to achieve Christian unity, institutionally or doctrinally, we can now already be joined in prayers, an anticipation of our praying together in heaven.

119

Morning and evening prayer's reliance on Scriptures is part of this. For all our differences, Christians agree on the centrality of Scriptures. Therefore Christians of many different stripes and traditions can share biblical prayer widely.

In visits to ecumenical communities with international influence—Iona, Taizé, Northumbria—I saw that their daily morning and evening prayer involves Christians and traditions from all confessions around the world. Members and guests alike often commented on the significance of this.

. A lifelong Baptist at Northumbria told me of her original discomfort with liturgical worship. But now she especially appreciated that daily fixed-hour prayer gave her a connection with other Christians and the richness of their traditions.

Such prayer is the only Roman Catholic liturgy in which all Christians may fully participate. In May, 2000, Roman Catholic and Anglican bishops (from thirteen areas of the world) had a historic weeklong conference in Mississauga, Ontario, on possible reunification. While much divided them, they commented on the delight of their "sense of sameness discovered through actions like the daily ritual of morning and evening prayer. . . ." Cardinal Edward Idris Cassidy, president of the Vatican's Pontifical Council for Promoting Christian Unity, commented: "We have been together . . . in morning and evening prayer. . . . We are fully in communion in prayer."[11]

THE GIFTS OF SOLIDARITY AND SUPPORT

Christians have the option of the solidarity of praying similar words and themes with other Christians. When I traveled in the British Isles, I was struck by the "dispersed communities" of Iona, Northumbria, and Aidan and Hilda. Each community is made up of people who live apart from one another but have made mutual promises about lifestyles, priorities, and ways to be accountable to one another for these. A primary commitment is shared daily prayer. People are sustained in faithfulness by being prayerfully connected.

Christian prayer is intended to be corporate. The only prayer Jesus gave us begins with "our"; we find there "we" and "us," but not "mine," "I," or "me." Common prayer means we intentionally join in prayer with others.

I tried hard to pray for years, but found it hard to keep my discipline. Yet when I vowed before monks at St. Gregory's Abbey, I made great strides in discipline. I was better able to pray regularly, not just because I took a vow to do so, but also because I knew that brother monks at St. Gregory's Abbey were praying with me and for me.

An example from another sphere of my life illustrates this. Some years ago I joined a writers' group. Their perspectives improved my work. They kept me accountable, as it was regularly my turn to share work with them. Thus I had to produce. Besides, writing—like prayer— can be devastatingly solitary. One sits in front of a blank computer screen or a blank page and wonders, "Why do I bother?" There are times when prayer feels the same way: lonely, blank, and pointless too. But just knowing that there were others in my writers' group—in the town where I lived—struggling with the same issues, encouraged me to keep going. Not coincidentally, I completed my first book within a year of joining the group. In the spiritual life, as in writing, it is a gift to draw upon and practice disciplines in solidarity and community with others.

Someone said that those who pray with the support of others are like mountain climbers roped together. Those who pray alone are like individual pioneers who learn by trial and error, without the help, support, and guidance of others who have gone ahead. With a common discipline or Office, we move beyond privatized, "personal devotions" to praying with other believers, not only around the world but also with the communion of saints. The Office reminds us that no matter what our race, country, location, denomination, or liturgical preference might happen to be, as Christians we have more in common than not.

A former parishioner learned the value of mutual connection, commitment, and support in an unexpected way. She joined the Easter season project where a small group committed themselves to daily morning and evening prayer. Her husband was traveling two or more weeks a month overseas. They each bought the prayer book, both saying it was not their "style." During their regular separations, though, this shared discipline was a strong connection as they e-mailed back and forth commentaries and reflections on the readings and prayers of the day.

Solidarity and communion in common prayer operates several ways.

It gives support and encouragement in prayers. A friend visited a monastery. He told me that the often repeated doxology—"Glory to the Father, and to the Son, and to the Holy Spirit, as it was in the beginning, is now and will be forever"—gave him comfort. Whenever he remembered the monks praying that, he would pray it too and take heart.

Common prayer even brings unity where we might not want it. At times, I was involved in prayers where someone was present whom I disliked or with whom I was in conflict. I would not have chosen to have that person there. But God's wisdom works differently from ours. I learned that I could even pray with people with whom I disagree. (It would probably be harder for both parties if that person or I made up our own prayers, but following a program was helpful.) Morning and evening prayer is especially challenging here when we say, "Forgive us our sins, as we forgive those who sin against us." Intriguingly, this was one reason that Benedict wanted the Lord's Prayer prayed every morning and evening: so that monks would remember the importance of mutual forgiveness.

Prayer is hard to do without others' support. Brother Émile told me:

> People are not going to be able to persevere in personal prayer. In regular common prayer, you join together and take your part—every week, month, or day. Discouragement is too easy today. But in common prayer you support one another. We are never all at the same place during any time. This week I support you and next week I need your support.

TWO-WAY BLESSINGS

We praise and worship God because God is worthy of praise and worship. ("Worship" literally means "ascribing worth.") God calls us to such worship, and probably nothing further need be said. This in itself is argument enough for daily morning and evening prayer. But the truth is that our praise and worship of God brings many blessings, as we saw in this chapter when we looked at the gifts and blessings of common morning and evening prayer.

When I did a pulpit exchange in the Netherlands, a parishioner there asked me about the word "blessing."

In Dutch, the word is "zegen." But in Dutch, only people can be blessed. Blessing is divine, conferred by God. This parishioner was confused about how "blessing" is used in English, especially when we speak of "blessing God." The English understanding of the word is broader and includes the sense of thanking, praising, glorifying, and adoring—all primary elements of the liturgy of the hours.

I am fond of Dutch, my mother tongue, but here I prefer English. Because the truth is that blessings are seldom one-way. If I live and minister in a way that blesses or brings blessing to others at home, in the seminary, and at church, then I know that I am often blessed in the process. People who minister and serve others often say that they feel blessed in what they do.

Prayer and worship also work in this two-way fashion. In blessing God with prayers and offerings (a word closely related to "office"), we experience blessings. The process goes on and on, since as we bless God because of the blessings we receive, then we have all the more reason to praise and be thankful.

The Office can certainly be hard to pray, and it has its challenges, to be sure, yet it is hard not to be enthusiastic about it. In God's paradoxical and upside-down economy, the cost is often its own reward.

CHAPTER 9

Testing the Waters

Experiments in Praying Morning and Evening Prayer

SHEILA'S LIFE FELL APART. She was a lifelong Christian with dreams of a family, secure work, and a reliable income, yet in a few months she lost almost everything. Separated from her spouse, not by her choice or preference, she moved away from her children and the family home into an ugly, cheaply furnished apartment, all alone. Time passed slowly. Furthermore, she had trouble holding ·down regular work and so also experienced economic insecurity.

Without work or family, Sheila had little in the way of structure, rhythm, or purpose. During this time, she learned for the first time about fixed-hour prayer. Prayer and Bible reading were always important for her. Yet she was never able to maintain a regular discipline.

In the midst of her troubles, she began to pray every morning and evening. Scriptures came alive as she read and prayed them in the midst of her own life. She had a lot to talk over with God.

Then she noticed something. A church in town daily rang bells at regular intervals. They had always rung, but she never noticed them before. Now that she knew about common prayer, she recognized them as a call to prayer. And she took heart, even though she was not even completely sure *which* church it was.

In trying circumstances, Sheila was ministered to by an often overlooked and often ignored Christian tradition, fixed-hour prayer, as she practiced it privately and was encouraged in it by the wider church.

IF WE TRY IT, WILL THEY LIKE IT?

I love ideas and dreaming. In elementary school, I sometimes got into trouble because I had trouble paying attention to what happened in class or was said by the teacher. I spent a lot of time looking out the window and getting lost in fantasies. So it is important to test my ideas, theories, and theology.

As a pastor, I wanted to know whether these ideas about fixed-hour prayer could be implemented. So one year, in my former congregation during the season of Easter until Pentecost, a dozen people committed themselves to praying common morning and evening prayer five times a week, using a favorite prayerbook, *Companion to the Breviary.* People filled out questionnaires and kept spiritual journals to help me understand what this experience was like. As well, we gathered on Wednesdays to pray evening prayers together and recaptured a lost tradition of Wednesday night prayer meetings. We also shared about how the project was going, and I taught the group about the Office's history and theology, about developing prayer disciplines, and about the challenges of being prayerful in our busy lives.

This was a rewarding enterprise for the pastor and the parishioners alike.

People learned a lot and acquired a new way to pray, and many commented on how this experience challenged them to be more disciplined in prayer. Some said they had never before considered spending this much time praying, but they found that twenty to thirty minutes was quite doable. Here too was the person that I mentioned earlier, the one who was able to pray for the first time since a family tragedy over two years earlier.

Some struggled with an "imposed prayer" of so many words. But others who could never previously maintain prayer now could. Several were pleasantly surprised to be able to keep this discipline. One learned so much from this way of praying that she used its praise–listening–response outline to structure spontaneous prayers. Most grew comfortable with it. Some saw it works well in a busy lifestyle. One was surprised at how easy it was.

By the end of our time together, most said they would not continue common prayer twice a day but would spend more time praying in the future. Over a year later, four people still regularly used the prayer book. Everyone in the group told me at first of their longing for spiritual growth, and this experience motivated them to be more deliberate in their prayer life.

Towards the end of our time, I had several offers from people outside the group to buy any prayer books that project participants no longer wanted. But none wanted to sell their books. Several planned to use theirs in the morning or evening, and one wanted to use it in her upcoming retirement. Some started thinking about shaping an Office that took into consideration our own Mennonite church history, traditions, and hymns.

One thing that struck people was how commitment to others and praying with others helped them maintain a discipline. One said: "If I hadn't promised to do this, I wouldn't make it." They wondered how the church could keep encouraging and supporting people to pray together.

Another benefit of our practice was that people reflected much on psalms because fixed-hour prayer relies heavily on them. One person entered saying she hated the psalms, but she and others studied a Walter Brueggemann book on psalms for more perspective. Several wanted more psalms in worship and dreamed about learning to sing them. They came to a new appreciation. Another wrote in her journal, "Praying psalms which often recite salvation history gives me a sense of being part of a long history of struggle and mercy. My struggles are a small bit of this broad story, which leads to hope and trust in God's guidance and mercy." One called this a good "practice to ground myself in Christian identity."

Many noticed that this way of praying affected daily life. One said, "I feel more grateful for each day, and am more aware of God's goodness as I read the psalms and prayers." Another said that it "made me more aware of God's constant presence." Others spoke of having a greater sense of purpose and direction. One was helped to pray for a wider range of concerns than usual. Still another wrote in her journal, "In daily prayer there is recurring longing to live truthfully, justly, according to God's call in my life." Someone else said: "Frequently words from Scripture stayed with me throughout the day."

One spoke of how this worked in a busy life: "The daily prayer was helpful because it reminded me to stop and read and pray." Another said, "Sometimes it was just going through the motions, especially at night when I was tired. I still think it was okay: a sleepy good night to God, but a turning of intention nonetheless." This person was strongly helped by the prayers: "Some days I felt so calm and centered, like I was balanced on the edge of something (a tightrope, a pin), and the feeling of balance stayed a long time."

Some felt freed. They no longer had to figure everything out: what, when, or for how long to pray. One said: "It was all there, I didn't need to look any further." Another observed, "I could just read it over and get as much out of it as possible." One summarized it this way: "The Office covers it all efficiently. I don't have to be worried that I've missed something. It's measurable. I know when I'm done and thus have freedom from guilt." Many said this helped them to pray more.

There were implications for worship. Several now felt better prepared for Sundays. One said that daily prayers made "Sunday worship seem less out of sync with the rest of life." Another noted that fixed-hour prayer is not as "I-centered" as some contemporary worship. Several said that the Easter *season* (not normally stressed by Mennonites) now had deeper meaning.

This experience also created appropriate dissatisfaction. Some were now less happy with how they had prayed before. One had never thought before of praying every evening.

I do not pretend that people loved everything. This was obviously not the case, as most did not commit themselves to it over the long term. One perplexing thing was that often the thing one person most liked (e.g,. psalms or repetition) was also the very thing someone else least liked. This reminds us that such prayer does not work the same for all. Furthermore, it suggests that common prayer—like Sunday worship—works best if it is sufficiently varied to help people engage in different ways.

By the end of our time, several said that they would miss having others praying at similar times, with the same content, and praying for each other.

While many began with some suspicion of this way of praying, by the end most rated this experience of prayer as "good." Several commented on how much they liked and felt comfortable with the Office.

This small experiment confirms the importance of churches finding and generating ways to meet people's need to pray, to call and remind people to pray regularly, and to build a sense of praying along with others.

Such prayer can be hard—as shown in struggles that were discussed in sharing times and in journals. A fervent Office *advocate* says this is the hardest form of prayer. Yet some who could never previously maintain prayer learned a new way to pray and were surprised to see that they were able to keep this discipline. Several saw for the first time that commitment and discipline are possible. Some commented that the Office is achievable, for some even easy. One wrote in the last questionnaire:

> It suddenly seems to me there's really no excuse. It still felt calm and relaxed. I think I'll keep on going [after this project]. I like this book [the *Breviary*].

(A year later, this participant was still praying the office—and this from a person who previously found it difficult to maintain a daily discipline.)

People gave serious (and often new) thought about how to pray. Even those who did not continue using the Breviary resolved to spend more time with other ways of praying. This common prayer encouraged a longing for spiritual growth; it motivated people to work on and improve prayer.

Thus I urge churches to find more ways to meet people's need to pray, and to call and remind people to pray regularly every day. This kind of prayer was not suitable for everyone in the study group, so I do not suggest that it should be imposed as an obligation on all Christians. Even eloquent advocates of fixed-hour prayer admit it is not for everyone. Yet it is deeply rooted in the New Testament church, and needs and deserves more attention.

This "lost treasure" of daily morning and evening prayer had much to offer a small group that had known virtually nothing about it before. They were pleasantly surprised by many discoveries, their faith was enriched, and their prayer was enhanced. Many could benefit by uncovering fixed-hour prayer, an important heritage of all Christians.

LAST WORDS

Sheila discovered the deeper meaning of the familiar sound of church bells as a reminder of God's presence, call, and invitation to pray. There is an old Anglican tradition that bells are rung when common prayer begins. Not only are they a call to prayer, but also they can be a loving gesture to tell one's neighbors that they too are in our prayers.

There are other ways to invite people into our prayers. On a special occasion, David Adam wrote a prayer about his island community and distributed it in the town. Many neighbors posted it in their homes and prayed it when they heard the bell. They found it significant even as a discipline for just a few weeks. Others continued to use it for a long time.

In a time of pilgrimage and seeking, when people look to ancient Christian resources—or elsewhere when we do not provide them—and struggle with deep questions, the church needs to provide refuges of prayer and help people by providing structures and support for prayer.

John Westerhoff III and William Willimon discuss the challenge of recovering daily prayer.

If the Church does nothing else for the world other than to keep open a house, symbolic of the home-land of the soul, where in-season and out-of-season people can gather daily to pray, it is doing the social order the greatest possible service. So long as the Church bids people to daily meditation and prayer, and provides a simple and credible vehicle for the devotional life, it need not question its place, mission, and influence in the world. If it loses faith in the daily offering of common prayer, it need not look to its avocations to save it, for it is dead at heart.

Nothing may be more important than a rebirth of daily morning and evening common prayer in every church.[1]

Once I would have considered their conclusion to be exaggerated, but my own practice, work with parishioners, travel to European communities, and theological reflections, convince me that they are right.

By uncovering this lost treasure, the church takes one more step toward the vision of the psalmist who proclaimed,

From the rising of the sun to its setting
praised be the name of the Lord. (113:3)[2]

Tips for Praying Morning and Evening Prayer

I DO NOT RECOMMEND making up one's own office of morning and evening prayer. In Appendix D, "Choosing a Prayer Book", there is advice on how to select an appropriate one. In the section called "Recommended Resources for Morning and Evening Prayer", you will also find counsel on whether the books are better suited for individuals or groups.

For those not accustomed to fixed-hour prayers, the following suggestions might provide a place to start.

FINDING YOUR WAY, LEARNING THE STRUCTURE

If you or the members of your group struggle with how to proceed or find your way in a chosen prayer book, look first to see if there are instructions in the book itself. Many prayer books have helps or guides near the beginning.

Look also at Appendix B in this book on the "Structure and Content of Morning and Evening Prayer." This will help you understand the order. Chances are that when you know the structure of the prayers, your prayer book will suddenly make a lot more sense and will be much less confusing.

By the way, in many prayer books, Saturday evening prayer is labeled "Sunday Evening I." (Sunday evening, as we normally understand it, is "Sunday Evening II.")

It might also be helpful to know that particular days often have themes. Fridays recall Good Friday and are penitential. Saturdays have a tone of preparing us for Sunday worship. Sundays celebrate the Resurrection and so are joyful.

ENHANCING YOUR PRAYERS

You may want to take your tradition's hymnbook and find hymns particularly suited to morning and evening prayers. These can enrich your prayer. Often prayer books, for example Phyllis Tickle's volumes of *The Divine Hours*, suggest hymns.

If possible, try to pray your prayers at approximately the same time, when you can be relatively free of disturbances or interruptions and can ignore the phone.

Many also find it helpful to set aside a special place for their prayer. Such a place (it need not be a room; a corner, a cushion, or a chair will do) should be visually conducive to prayer. One can add a flower, a candle, a rock, an icon, or a piece of art to enhance the worshipful quality. Try not to be in a place that is cluttered or that reminds you of all the work you have to do.

START MODESTLY

Many prayer sequences can be prayed in 10 to 15 minutes. It is better to begin shorter and slowly expand as you desire, than to begin too ambitiously and get discouraged. The length of your prayers will depend on whether you add periods of silence or spend time in free prayer, conversing with God. Some prayer books give ideas about where to include silences. Pray slowly and deliberately.

By the way, C.W. McPherson, in his excellent book, recommends beginning with either morning or evening prayer for a time, perhaps several weeks or months, before trying to do both regularly.[1] It is too hard to go from not saying common prayer to then saying it twice a day. You may risk being frustrated and discouraged, and you might give up entirely. Start shorter and build as you can.

If you are by yourself, do not feel compelled to do everything at a steady pace. John Brook recommends, "If a phrase or word catches you, stay with it, savour its meaning before moving on." In so doing you honor the Spirit's prompting and your own prayer happens.[2] Consider memorizing a short phrase (as little as three or four words) from those prayers and carrying it with you through the rest of your day.

At the end of your prayers, do not rush off. Bask in the silence and refreshment for a few moments.

PRAYING WITH SCRIPTURES

Remember that the prayers are mostly Scriptures. Office prayer books are a way of using Scriptures to pray, pay attention to God, listen to God, check our lives and bearings alongside Scriptures, interpret our lives by Scripture, and ask God to mold our hearts and lives by God's priorities.

I recommend saying—or even chanting—psalms and canticles aloud. One resource can help: Cynthia Bourgeault's tapes *Singing the Psalms: How to Chant in the Christian Contemplative Tradition.* (See "Recommended Resources for Morning and Evening Prayer.") We move more deeply into their meaning when the texts are oral, not silent. (In earlier centuries, all reading was done out loud.) It is also easier to memorize texts read aloud than ones read silently.

Psalms and canticles often include an antiphon to be said before and after the recitation. This short phrase emphasizes a certain theme in the text.

Usually after the psalms, the prayer includes the Gloria Patri: "Glory to the Father, and to the Son, and to the Holy Spirit. As it was in the beginning, is now, and will be for ever. Amen." The Gloria Patri goes back at least as early as the fourth century and reminds

140

us that our prayers are actually praise.[3] Some Christian communities now pray a different version: "Glory to you, Source of all Being, Eternal Word and Holy Spirit, as it was in the beginning, is now, and will be forever. Amen."

After the Scripture readings, I recommend pausing in silence for at least three to five minutes and pondering what God might be saying to you through that text this day. Discuss with God what you hear.

Following the Gospel reading there is often a responsory that focuses on a theme from the Scripture reading.

INTERCESSIONS

When praying intercessions, alone or in a group, pause between petitions to name silently or aloud concerns that come to mind. Also give yourself time to incorporate your own prayer list. It is important to close this time of prayer with the Lord's Prayer, as Christians have done for two millennia.

THINK LIKE A CHOIR—PRAYING IN A GROUP

To get a sense of how to pray this way in a group, consider visiting a monastery, a local church, or another Christian community with fixed-hour prayers. While you may not wish to imitate everything they do, the atmosphere will be instructive, and you may pick up practical tips.

One more pointer: If you are saying prayers in a group, be mindful of the persons praying around you. Just as when singing in a choir, it is important to keep pace with each other and not to outdo each other in volume.

If you are fortunate enough to have a group committed to praying common prayer, try to join together at least once a week. Such gatherings not only reinforce and deepen our commitment, they remind us that our prayers are common. Taizé brothers kept reminding me how hard it is to maintain such prayer disciplines without the regular support of others.

Structure and Content of Morning and Evening Prayer

IT IS GOOD TO UNDERSTAND the flow or plot of the Office. Morning and evening prayer evolved and were passed down with a parallel threefold order: praise of God (psalms or hymns), listening to God's Word (usually the day's Gospel reading), and responding to God's Word (silence, a creed, a hymn or a canticle, *and* intercessions). The response always includes the Lord's Prayer, a tradition that goes back to the earliest days of the church. Then the Office ends with a blessing.

The outline below is general and may vary somewhat in different Christian traditions. The content may not all be exactly the same, but the order will be similar, and certain key elements will appear in most if not all.

Most Offices have a psalm schedule, often near the end of the book. Moreover, there are various lectionary schemes for knowing which additional Scriptures to read on a given day. Sometimes (as in *The Book of Common Prayer*) the suggestions are in the book. Often your denomination will supply a list of suggested daily Scripture readings.

Address God in Praise	Morning Prayer	Evening Prayer
Invitation to Prayer	O Lord, open our lips. And our mouth shall declare your praise.	O God, make speed to save us. O Lord, make haste to help us.
		Glory to the Father, and to the Son, and to the Holy Spirit. As it was in the beginning, is now, and will be for ever. Amen.
Invitatory Psalm	Psalm 95, 96, 100, 67, 24.	
	Hymn	Hymn (possibly with theme of light)
	Prayer for Morning	Prayer for Evening
	Psalm: e.g., Psalm 3, 5, 57,	Evening Psalm: e.g., Psalm 141, 92, 143, 63, 664, 16
Listen to God		
	Scripture Lessons	Scripture Lessons
	Old Testament Canticle	New Testament Canticle
	Gospel	Tomorrow's Gospel
	Silence	Silence
Respond to God		

Address . . . continued	Morning . . . continued	Evening . . . continued
	Zechariah's Cantivcle (Benedictus)	Mary's Canticle (Magnificat)
	Intercessions (dedicating day)	Intercessions (for the world's needs)
	Lord's Prayer	Lord's Prayer
	Collect	Collect
	Blessing and Dismissal	Blessing and Dismissal

Preparing a Space for Corporate Celebration

WHEN I MET WITH Brother Émile of Taizé, he spoke of the importance of paying attention to preparing and setting up for worship and prayer. He noted the irony that we are deliberate in getting meals ready and making a hospitable space when we entertain: "How much care do we take for prayer, the singing, the place? What do we do to make it inviting, warm? The place of prayer says a lot."

I am not visually oriented, but as a pastor I often saw that attention to visual details makes a huge difference to many people's engagement in worship. Once, my wife and I were looking for a new church and attended a service that impressed us greatly. But afterwards she surprised me when she said she could not regularly attend there. Why not, I wondered. "That sanctuary is too ugly. I'd find it depressing," she responded. In that moment, I saw the importance of paying attention to our worship space.

What is important when setting up for corporate worship? Several practical details are worth noting:

- Consider using a church or another place with sacred associations. Praying between prayer-drenched walls not only deepens a sense of reverence, but also is a physical connection with those who have prayed there before.

- Whether or not the room has sacred associations, you can heighten the worshipful quality of the space by placing a simple religious object or two in it: a cross, a Bible, candles, art, or icons. Keep it simple and do not have too many objects. Cluttered spaces distract from what is central.

- Seating can be lined up or curved, facing a focal worship center (a cross, a table) or arranged so that worshipers face each other. What you choose may depend on your theology. Do you want to make a priority of facing those in the community, or should you corporately face away from yourselves and toward a focal worship point? Monastics pray facing each other. This arrangement also works in my own, more congregational theology: The advantage of facing each other is that the sense of community and mutual encouragement is heightened.

- There should be light adequate enough for reading, but not too bright. Candles create warm light.

- Have a sufficient number of extra copies of your Office available for guests.

- Make sure that someone is available to orient guests by showing them how to use the materials and where the prayers are found.

Choosing a Prayer Book

WHEN I CONSIDER recommending an Office, I have two sets of criteria in mind. (See "Recommended Resources for Morning and Evening Prayer" for possibilities.)

PRACTICAL CONSIDERATIONS

Some criteria are practical.

- I like a book that is a good size for portability. Large, unwieldy books are hard to carry around and are even worse for traveling. (Actually I use one Office when at home and a smaller one while traveling, both because of the issue of portability and because when I travel I do not always have as much time to pray as when I am at home.)
- Unless one is highly motivated, it is best not to have a book with a large number of ribbons that need much puzzling out and searching as to what happens next. Happily, many new prayer books are laid out in easy-to-follow sections.
- Affordability is also an advantage.
- The book should be attractive looking, as this reminds us that what we are doing is worthwhile.
- The book should have a good binding that will

stand up to repeated use. It is helpful if it is bound in such a way that it falls open easily and lies flat without breaking the spine.

THEOLOGICAL CONCERNS

The other criteria are theological.

- If your own Christian tradition has an Office, that is the first place to look. (See Recommended Resources.)
- The prayer book needs to use a lot of Scripture in a good scholarly translation, preferably one that keeps inclusive language in mind. It is possible and hospitable to be inclusive without distorting the intent of the Scriptures.
- It is important to have a good translation of the psalms that retains the poetic rhythm. Not only were the psalms originally poetry, but they are difficult to pray constantly as mere prose.
- I prefer that the book be deeply rooted in Christian tradition (see Appendix B, Structure and Content of Morning and Evening Prayer).
- Books based in a community's life remind us that this prayer is common with that of other believers and so are preferable to individually authored examples.

Notes

CHAPTER 1: FINDING A LOST TREASURE

1 Douglas Van Steere, *Together in Solitude* (New York: Crossroad, 1982), p. 25.

2 C.W. McPherson, *Grace at this Time: Praying the Daily Office* (Harrisburg, PA: Morehouse, 1999), p. 1.

3 This version tends to be used by Anglicans. See for example the Society of Saint Francis's *Celebrating Common Prayer* (New York: Mowbray, 1992), p. 13.

4 Unless otherwise noted, Scripture citations are from the *New Revised Standard Version*.

5 *Celebrating Common Prayer*, p. 28.

6 These translations are from The Episcopal Church's *The Book of Common Prayer* (New York: Seabury, 1979), pp. 115–116.

7 Shelvia Dancy, "Fixed-hour Prayer Moving Out of the Monastery," *Religion News Service*, May 30, 2000, pp. 3–5; Heidi Schlumpf, "Teach Me to Pray," *Publishers Weekly*, May 29, 2000, p. S9. Some information is also taken from Tickle phone interviews, September 25–26, 2000.

8 Frances R. Havergal, "Take my Life," in *Hymnal: A Worship Book* (Scottdale, PA: Herald Press, 1992), p. 389.

CHAPTER 3: ANCIENT RHYTHMS OF PRAYER

1 Suzanne Guthrie, *Praying the Hours* (Cambridge, MA: Cowley, 2000), p. 67.

2 D.H. Farmer, ed., "The Voyage of St. Brendan," in *The Age of Bede*, trans. J.F. Webb (New York: Penguin Books, 1998), p. 243.

3   See my *On Earth as in Heaven: A New Look at the Lord's Prayer* (Scottdale, PA: Herald, 1992).

4   Joachim Jeremias, *The Prayers of Jesus*, trans. John Bowden et al. (Philadelphia: Fortress, 1967), pp. 77–78.

5   John Brook, *The School of Prayer: An Introduction to the Divine Office for All Christians* (Collegeville, MN: Liturgical Press, 1992), p. 9.

CHAPTER 4: WHERE HAVE ALL THE HOURS GONE?

1   Paul Bradshaw, *Two Ways of Praying* (Nashville: Abingdon, 1995), pp. 17–21. We do not look at all his contrasts here.

2   Roger S. Wieck, *Time Sanctified: The Book of Hours in Medieval Art and Life* (New York: George Braziller, 1988), p. 27.

3   Information and quotes in this paragraph are from J. Neil Alexander, "Luther's Reform of the Daily Office," *Worship* 57, no. 4 (July 1983), pp. 349–351, 359.

4   Paul Bradshaw, "Whatever Happened to Daily Prayer?" *Worship* 64, no. 1 (January 1990), p. 19. Eamon Duffy suggests that the English Reformation greatly harmed the personal prayer practices of many laypersons: "When all is said and done, the Reformation was a violent disruption, not the natural fulfillment, of most of what was vigorous in late medieval piety and religious practice." *The Stripping of the Altars: Traditional Religion in England, c. 1400–c. 1580* (New Haven: Yale University Press, 1992), p. 4.

5   Quotes and ideas in this paragraph are from Bradshaw, *Two Ways of Praying*, pp. 36, 40–41.

6   John Rempel, ed., *Minister's Manual* (Scottdale, PA: Herald, 1998), p. 15.

7   John H. Yoder, trans. and ed., *The Legacy of Michael Sattler* (Scottdale, PA: Herald, 1973), p. 44, 54 n. 105.

8   McClendon, *Balthasar Hubmaier, Catholic Anabaptist*, 73. See also Torsten Bergsten, *Balthasar Hubmaier: Anabaptist Theologian and Martyr*, trans. W.R. Estep, Jr. (Valley Forge: Judson, 1978), p. 325, 545 n. 24.

9   Marion Kobelt-Groch, "Why Did Petronella Leave her Husband? Reflections on Marital Avoidance Among the Halberstadt Anabaptists," *Mennonite Quarterly Review* 62, no. 1 (January 1988), p. 27.

10 Claus-Peter Clasen, *Anabaptism: A Social History* (Ithaca: Cornell University Press, 1972), p. 276.

11 Information in this paragraph is derived from *Mennonite Encyclopedia*, vol. IV, s.v. "Prayer Books, Mennonite," p. 211, and Robert Friedmann, *Mennonite Piety Through the Centuries* (Scottdale, PA: Mennonite Publishing House, 1949).

CHAPTER 5: TAKE OUR MOMENTS AND OUR DAYS

1   Dorotheos of Gaza, *Discourses and Sayings: Desert Humor and Humility*, trans. Eric P. Wheeler (Kalamazoo, MI: Cistercian Publications, 1977), pp. 176–177.

2   Clyde Edgerton, *Walking Across Egypt* (New York: Ballantine Books, 1987), p. 82.

3   Wendy M. Wright, *The Time Between: Cycles and Rhythms in Ordinary Time* (Nashville: Upper Room, 2000), p. 30.

4   John Cassian, *The Conferences*, trans. Boniface Ramsey (New York: Paulist, 1997), pp. 739–740.

5   Eugene H. Peterson, *Working the Angles: The Shape of Pastoral Integrity* (Grand Rapids, MI: Eerdmans, 1987), p. 48.

6   Dorothy Bass, *Receiving the Day: Christian Practices for Opening the Gift of Time* (San Francisco: Jossey-Bass, 2000), p. 12.

7   Donna Schaper, *Sabbath Keeping* (Cambridge, MA: Cowley, 1999), pp. 9, 10.

8   George Guiver, *Company of Voices: Daily Prayer and the People of God* (New York: Pueblo, 1988), p. 15.

9   As cited in John Brook, *The School of Prayer: An Introduction to the Divine Office for All Christians* (Collegeville, MN: Liturgical Press, 1992), pp. 5–6.

10 Charles Cummings, *Monastic Practices* (Kalamazoo, MI: Cistercian Publications, 1986), pp. 78–79.

CHAPTER 6: THE FREEDOM OF DISCIPLINES

1 "Equal Time for Norwegian Atheists," *Christian Century*, vol. 117 #13, April 19–26, 2000, pp. 453–454.

2 William Dalrymple, *From the Holy Mountain: A Journey in the Shadow of Byzantium* (London: HarperCollins, 1998), p. 168.

3 Timothy Fry, ed., RB 1980: *The Rule of St. Benedict* (Collegeville, MN: Liturgical Press, 1981), pp. 215, 217.

4 Cited in "Reflections" Column, *Christianity Today*, October 22, 1990, p. 43.

5 *The Sayings of the Desert Fathers*, trans. Benedicta Ward (Kalamazoo MI: Cistercian Publications, 1975), pp. 3–4.

CHAPTER 7: WRESTLING FOR A BLESSING

1 Robert Ellsberg, *All Saints: Daily Reflections on Saints, Prophets, and Witnesses for Our Time* (New York: Crossroad, 1997), p. 261.

2 Dietrich Bonhoeffer, *Life Together*, trans. John W. Doberstein (New York: Harper & Row, 1954), p. 64.

3 Quotes and ideas in this paragraph are from William H. Willimon and Stanley Hauerwas, *Lord, Teach Us: The Lord's Prayer and the Christian Life* (Nashville: Abingdon, 1996), pp. 16–20.

4 Joan Chittister, *Wisdom Distilled from the Daily: Living the Rule of St. Benedict Today* (San Francisco: Harper, 1991), p. 31.

5 Yushi Nomura, *Desert Wisdom: Sayings from the Desert Fathers* (New York: Doubleday, 1982), p. 59.

6 David Adam interview.

7 As quoted by Debra K. Farrington, *Living Faith Day by Day* (New York: Perigee, 2000), p. 81.

8 C.W. McPherson, *Grace at this Time: Praying the Daily Office* (Harrisburg, PA: Morehouse, 1999), p. 87.

CHAPTER 8: GIVING AT THE OFFICE

1 Richard J. Foster, *Prayer: Finding the Heart's True Home* (San Francisco: HarperCollins, 1992), p. 106.

2 Richard J. Foster, *Prayer: Finding the Heart's True Home*, pp. 107–108.

3 Mark Galli, "Memorable Speech," *Christianity Today*, January 8, 2001, p. 9.

4 John Brook, *The School of Prayer: An Introduction to the Divine Office for All Christians* (Collegeville, MN: Liturgical Press, 1992), pp. 3–4.

5 Lisa Belcher Hamilton, *For Those We Love But See No Longer: Daily Offices for Times of Grief* (Brewster, MA: Paraclete Press, 2001), p. xv.

6 Eugene H. Peterson, *Under the Unpredictable Plant: An Exploration in Vocational Holiness* (Grand Rapids, MI: Eerdmans, 1992), p. 101.

7 Eugene H. Peterson, *Under the Unpredictable Plant: An Exploration in Vocational Holiness*, pp. 102–103.

8 John Brook, *The School of Prayer: An Introduction to the Divine Office for All Christians*, p. 89.

9 Gary Cross, *Time and Money: The Making of Consumer Culture* (New York: Routledge, 1993), p. 1.

10 Esther Quinlan, "Sailing Home," *Sacred Journey* 52, no. 4, August 2001, pp. 33, 37.

11 Kerry Kelly, "Laying the Cornerstone for Christian Unity," *Catholic New Times*, June 11, 2000, p. 12.

CHAPTER 9: TESTING THE WATERS

1 John H. Westerhoff III and William H. Willimon, *Liturgy and Learning Through the Life Cycle* (Akron, OH: OSL Publications, 1994), p. 81.

2 *The Grail Psalms: Singing Version* (London: Collins, 1963).

APPENDIX A

1 C.W. McPherson, *Grace at this Time: Praying the Daily Office* (Harrisburg, PA: Morehouse, 1999), p. 90.

2 John Brook, *The School of Prayer: An Introduction to the Divine Office for All Christians* (Collegeville, MN: Liturgical Press, 1992), p. 29.

3 C.W. McPherson, *Grace at this Time: Praying the Daily Office*, p. 28.

Recommended Resources for Morning and Evening Prayer

There are many excellent prayer books from various denominational streams.

- Anglican: Howard Galley, compiler and editor, expanded the *Book of Common Prayer* office and added readings and other devotional material in *The Prayer Book Office* (New York: The Church Hymnal Corporation, 1994). The Church of the Province of New Zealand (Anglican) has a wonderful *BCP* version, *A New Zealand Prayer Book: He Karakia Mihinare O Aotearo* (San Francisco: Harper, 1997).

- Lutheran: Frederick J. Schumacher and Dorthy A. Zelenko compiled and edited the comprehensive *For All the Saints: Prayer Book For and By the Church* (Delhi, NY: American Lutheran Publicity Bureau, 1996).

157

- Orthodox: These vary according to the various traditions. I like, for example, *The Agpeya: The Coptic Orthodox Prayer Book of the Hours*, Second Edition (Brooklyn: Coptic Orthodox Church of St. George, 1987).

- Presbyterian (USA): The *Book of Common Worship: Daily Prayer* (Louisville: Westminster/ John Knox, 1993) is excellent.

- Roman Catholic: The main version is *The Liturgy of the Hours* (New York: Catholic Book Publishing Company, 1975). This is a three-volume set, but it comes in an abridged one-volume version, *Christian Prayer: The Liturgy of the Hours* (New York: Catholic Book Publishing Company, 1976). I particularly like another condensed version, *A Shorter Morning and Evening Prayer: The Psalter of the Liturgy of the Hours* (Collegeville, MN: Liturgical Press, 1997).

- United Methodist: The Methodist Order of Saint Luke (OSL) has an Office edited by Timothy J. Crouch, *The Book of Offices and Services* (Akron, OH: Order of Saint Luke, 1994). It has more complete versions in a multivolume set, *Advent Through the Season of Epiphany*, vol. 1 (1998); *Lent*, vol. 2 (scheduled for publication in 2002); *The Great Fifty Days*, vol. 3 (2000); *Ordinary Time (First Half)*, vol. 4a (1997); *Ordinary Time (Second Half)*, vol. 4b

(1997); *For All the Saints*, vol. 5 (1995); *A Daily Lectionary*, vol. 6 (2001).

RECOMMENDED MORNING AND EVENING PRAYER BOOKS

Below are noteworthy prayer books. (In parentheses at the end of each entry, I note whether it is primarily recommended for individual use, corporate use, or both.)

- Adam, David. *The Rhythm of Life: Celtic Daily Prayer*. Harrisburg, PA: Morehouse, 1996.

  Adam has written a one-week cycle of four daily prayers. It is well done, and I particularly like to use it when traveling.

  (Individual)

- Benson, Robert. *Venite: A Book of Daily Prayer*. New York: Tarcher/Putnam, 2000.

  Benson found too many prayerbooks difficult to use, so he wrote a one-volume version for himself and was persuaded to share it with others. He includes four daily services and a helpful introduction on how to develop such a discipline. Actually, some ribbons would have been helpful.

  (Individual)

- Carmelites of Indianapolis. *People's Companion to the Breviary*. Two Volumes. Indianapolis: Carmelites of Indianapolis, 1997.

I recommend this more than any other. It is affordable and straightforwardly easy to use, and no ribbons
are needed. It includes selected spiritual readings, and
the intercessions alone are worth the price of the book.
Unlike many fixed-hour prayerbooks, this one works
hard at inclusive language. (I do not always approve
of how they rework psalms to be inclusive but—like
people—no prayerbook is perfect.)

These Carmelites also produced a good four-week
Psalter that can be used for common prayer,
*Companion to the Breviary: A Four-Week Psalter
with Intercessions*. Indianapolis: Carmelites of
Indianapolis, 1999.

(Individual/Corporate)

• Glenstal Abbey. *The Glenstal Book of Prayer: A
Benedictine Prayer Book*. Collegeville, MN:
Liturgical Press, 2001.

This is a simple, but traditional, prayerbook
developed by Benedictine monks in Ireland. While
beautifully laid out, it is a little short on variety.

(Individual/Corporate)

• Hamilton, Lisa Belcher. *For Those We Love But See
No Longer: Daily Offices for Times of Grief*.
Brewster, MA: Paraclete, 2001.

This "specialty office" was written with those
who grieve in mind. She organizes *Book of
Common Prayer* prayers into a one-week cycle of

four daily services. Its portable size makes it easy to carry and use anywhere.

(Individual)

- Newell, J. Philip. *Celtic Benediction: Morning and Night Prayer.* Grand Rapids, MI: Eerdmans, 2000. *Celtic Prayers From Iona.* New York: Paulist, 1997. *Sounds of the Eternal: A Celtic Psalter.* Grand Rapids: Eerdmans, 2002.

  Newell is a Church of Scotland pastor formerly associated with the Iona Community. His seven-day cycles of morning and evening prayers emphasize many Celtic themes. The books are all beautifully laid out and illustrated. The prayers are short and evocative. I would wish for deeper rootedness in Christian historical tradition and more reliance on Scriptures.

  (Individual)

- Raine, Andy, and John T. Skinner, eds. *Celtic Daily Prayer: A Northumbrian Office.* London: HarperCollins, 1994.

  This was designed for the Northumbria Community, a "dispersed community" in England. Northumbria was persuaded to publish it, and it has helped attract visitors and pilgrims from around the world. It incorporates Celtic themes, prayers, and saints.

  (Individual/Corporate)

- Society of St. Francis. *Celebrating Common Prayer.* New York: Mowbray, 1992.

  I use this prayer book, written by Anglican Franciscans in England. It is comprehensive and varied. For some it would be a little unwieldy: The book is large and requires many ribbons. I appreciate its elegance of language and structure and its firm rootedness in Christian tradition.
  (Individual/Corporate)

- Storey, William G. *An Everyday Book of Hours* and *A Seasonal Book of Hours.* Chicago: Liturgical Training Publications, 2001.

  Storey is a leading common prayer scholar who has been working for decades to promote accessible fixed-hour prayer. These books are fine examples: attractive, affordable, and easy to use.
  (Individual/Corporate)

- Sutera, Judith, ed. *Work of God.* Collegeville, MN: Liturgical Press, 1997.

  This is an attractive, compact, user-friendly, two-week cycle done in the Benedictine tradition. While there is much to commend about it, the psalm translations are not poetic enough.
  (Individual/Corporate)

- Tickle, Phyllis A. *The Divine Hours.* Three volumes: Autumn and Wintertime, Summertime, Springtime. New York: Doubleday, 2000, 2001.

These are elegant, lovely to hold, and simple to learn. Judging by sales, they are very popular. They are beautifully laid out and bound with good quality paper, and often include excellent hymn selections for evening prayer. They also have a nice introduction to the history of fixed-hour prayers, helpful instructions on praying in this manner, and even suggestions on how to chant.

(Individual)

- Webber, Robert. ed. and adapt. *The Prymer: The Prayer Book of the Medieval Era Adapted for Contemporary Use.* Brewster, MA: Paraclete Press, 2000.

  Robert Webber reprises a fifteenth-century prayerbook version of the Hours of the Blessed Virgin. This work also includes Prayers and Readings for a Time of Grief. Its focus on Mary will be off-putting for some.

  (Individual)

- Zimmerman, Joyce Ann, et al. *Pray without Ceasing: Prayer for Morning and Evening.* Collegeville, MN: Liturgical Press, 1993.

  This is an excellent prayer book. Scripture texts are carefully translated, with attention to inclusiveness. Canticles and intercessions are set to music. If the book were not so large and heavy, more people could use it.

  (Individual/Corporate)

RECOMMENDED RESOURCES ON MORNING
AND EVENING PRAYER

Below are books I particularly recommend that teach
about the Office.

• Cynthia Bourgeault, *Singing the Psalms: How to
Chant in the Christian Contemplative Tradition*
(Boulder, CO: Sounds True, 1997), three cassettes.
This is a charming—occasionally quirky—and
informative package that teaches both *how* and *why*
to chant the psalms. It contains a wealth of information about common prayer and even about *lectio
divina*, an ancient tradition of reading Scriptures
prayerfully.

• Bradshaw, Paul F. *Two Ways of Praying*. Nashville:
Abingdon, 1995.
Bradshaw, a leading worship scholar, shows how
church worship and private prayer became disconnected. He argues for reconnecting the two with a
reinvigorated Office.

• Brook, John. *The School of Prayer: An Introduction
to the Divine Office for All Christians*. Collegeville,
MN: Liturgical Press, 1992.
This is a useful handbook to the liturgy of the
hours: its theology, contents, and purposes.

• Guiver, George. *Company of Voices: Daily Prayer
and the People of God*. New York: Pueblo, 1988.

164

This is one of my favorite books on the history and theology of the Office, with lots of information and insights.

- Guthrie, Suzanne. *Praying the Hours.* Cambridge, MA: Cowley, 2000.

  This short, pleasantly written book reflects on the value of common prayer.

- McPherson, C.W. *Grace at this Time: Praying the Daily Office.* Harrisburg, PA: Morehouse, 1999.

  Written by an American Episcopal priest, this is the best and easiest-to-read introduction to the Office. Highly recommended.

- Taft, Robert. *The Liturgy of the Hours in East and West: The Origins of the Divine Office and Its Meaning for Today.* Collegeville, MN: Liturgical Press, 1986.

  If you want history and scholarship, this is the classic and indispensable text on understanding fixed-hour prayer.